Construction and Design Manual
Architectural Photography

Axel Hausberg, born in 1967, freelance photodesigner since 1998 focusing on architectural photography. Many exhibitions. Lives and works in Bad Neuenahr.

Anton Simons, born in 1960, journalist, blogger and book author. Lives and works in Sinzig/Rhein.

Christoph Gößmann, born in 1990, freelance photodesigner for architectural book publishers. Studied physics in Berlin.

Florian Meuser, born in 1975, freelance architect in Hong Kong. Engagements for architectural photography for international offices in China and South-East Asia.

Construction and Design Manual
Architectural Photography

Axel Hausberg / Anton Simons

With additional contributions by
Christoph Gößmann and Florian Meuser

DOM publishers

Contents

→ **PREFACE**
ARCHITECTURE AND PHOTOGRAPHY

- 8 — What is architectural photography
- 9 — What makes a good architectural photograph
- 10 — Who this book is aimed at
- 10 — How this book is structured

→ **CHAPTER 1**
THE HISTORY OF ARCHITECTURAL PHOTOGRAPHY

- 16 — Early technology
- 23 — The beginnings of architectural photography
- 26 — Pictorialism
- 34 — Straight photography
- 37 — *Neue Sachlichkeit*
- 45 — The postwar period

→ **CHAPTER 2**
OPTICAL PRINCIPLES

- 54 — Lenses and focal lengths
- 55 — Image circles
- 55 — Stitching
- 57 — 360-degree panoramas
- 57 — Shifting, swinging and tilting
- 57 — Framing and perspective
- 60 — Adjusting perspective
- 60 — Correcting horizontal lines
- 63 — Contrast
- 64 — High dynamic range imaging
- 68 — Resolution and sharpness
- 68 — Depth of field
- 71 — Increasing depth of field using the Scheimpflug principle

→ **CHAPTER 3**
EQUIPMENT

- 92 — Photographic disciplines
- 93 — Architectural photography with a small-format camera
- 95 — The view camera
- 97 — Digital backs
- 103 — Lenses for analogue and digital architectural photography
- 109 — The tripod
- 110 — The tripod head

CHAPTER 4
PHOTOGRAPHIC PRACTICE

- **119** — Realisation
- **136** — Light and lighting
- **166** — Exposure metering
- **169** — The RAW format

CHAPTER 5
COMPOSITION

- **173** — Subject
- **173** — Camera viewpoint, angle of view and distance from the subject
- **173** — Focal length
- **178** — Aperture and depth of field
- **178** — Image formats
- **178** — Foreground, middle distance and background
- **179** — The Golden Ratio
- **179** — The art of using lines

CHAPTER 6
POST-PROCESSING

- **196** — Developing
- **197** — Scanning
- **199** — Image editing
- **208** — Finishing

CHAPTER 7
COLOUR MANAGEMENT

- **224** — Camera calibration
- **225** — Calibration of the development process
- **225** — Monitor calibration
- **228** — Scanner calibration
- **228** — Printer calibration

CHAPTER 8
COMPOSITION AND ARTIFICIAL WORLDS, MODEL PHOTOGRAPHY, PHOTOGRAMMETRY

- **234** — Computer-generated imaging
- **234** — Photogrammetry
- **234** — Model photography

CHAPTER 9
EQUIPMENT TIPS

- **244** — Cameras
- **244** — Lenses
- **245** — Flash equipment
- **248** — Accessories
- **248** — Developing equipment
- **248** — Computers and monitors
- **248** — Scanner and scanning software
- **249** — Printers
- **249** — Image processing software

CHAPTER 10
EARNING MONEY FROM ARCHITECTURAL PHOTOGRAPHY

- **254** — Pathways into photography
- **256** — Tax and insurance
- **256** — Marketing
- **258** — Quotations, calculations, offers and orders
- **259** — Working with picture agencies
- **266** — Photographic right in practice using five legal cases

CHAPTER 11
APPENDIX

- **272** — Glossary
- **278** — Bibliography
- **280** — Directory of links
- **284** — Index

Preface
Architecture and photography

Axel Hausberg / Anton Simons

8 What is architectural photography?
9 What makes a good architectural photograph
10 Who this book is aimed at
10 How this book is structured

Anyone with a camera can take photographs of architecture. And because buildings tend to stay in the same place, architectural photographers have all the time in the world to press the shutter button – unlike their colleagues in news, fashion, wildlife and sports photography.

If architectural photography is so easy, why do we even need a book on the subject? We have written this manual because as architecture is not just about buildings, so architectural photography is not just about taking snapshots of them. Producing high-quality architectural photos requires large amounts of specialist knowledge and years of experience. It is one of the most demanding disciplines in photography, in terms of the quality of skills and equipment required, for three reasons:

1. <u>It must achieve exactly the right balance between the size of the subject, its distance from the camera, and the picture format. No other area of photography requires this.</u>

2. <u>Architectural photographs are often taken from off-centre viewpoints, sometimes out of necessity.</u>

3. <u>Lenses need to be calibrated very carefully.</u>

No other type of photography involves such a close relationship between the size of the subject and the image, and the height and distance from which it is taken. The subject, the photographer and the camera are intimately connected. Although this is also true of landscape photography, there the subject is usually so far away that the camera does not need to be tilted to adjust the perspective.

It is rarely possible to use central, half-height viewpoints for pictures of large buildings, and this often looks unnatural and even dull. For this reason, they are usually taken off-centre: for example, you would photograph a ten-storey building not from the fifth storey, but from eye level, tilting the camera upwards to fit the whole building in.

However, this creates unwanted converging lines which can be prevented only using a camera which corrects for perspective, and a lens with a far bigger image circle than the image on the sensor or film. Here again, with the exception of product photography, this makes it unique. On the other hand, the use of off-centre viewpoints creates the unique compositional opportunities that make architectural photography so interesting.

Every lens creates some distortion, making images slightly curved, particularly around the edges. This is not a problem with people, animals, landscapes, fashion and other images, but architecture is dominated by long straight lines, parallels and right angles, and photographs which do not exactly reproduce these can look unprofessional. Architectural photography therefore requires lenses with very large image circles and minimum distortion, which are expensive to design and manufacture. High-quality architectural photography demands specialist cameras and lenses, and specialist knowledge.

Sports, wildlife and news photographers can position themselves so that light falls at the right angle, and wait for exactly the right moment to press the shutter, while portrait and fashion photographers can pose their models. Here again, architectural photography is different. Since the subject does not move, the photographer has to find the right viewpoint for themself, regardless of the angle of the light. They therefore nearly always shoot from off-centre viewpoints, usually at eye level – which means having to deal with cars, rubbish bins, hedges and other obstacles and distractions. An adjacent neighbouring building may further reduce the choice of camera position, forcing the photographer to turn their back on it. And once they find a good viewpoint, they must then wait until the lights, mood and weather are just right, which may take weeks.

WHAT IS ARCHITECTURAL PHOTOGRAPHY?

It is defined as the process and product of planning, designing and construction. Modern man is surrounded almost continuously by architecture, and it affects his life even more than music, literature and painting.

Architectural photography is an art that represents three-dimensional architecture in two dimensions. It is a fast and effective way of capturing buildings separated by geography and time: allowing people to see buildings half a world away without going there, breaking down language barriers, and complementing or even replacing text. It is also an important teaching aid in the training of architects, urban planners and engineers, and one of the main tools of their trade. Architectural photography is one of the main ways in which innovative ideas about buildings spread so quickly across the world. It is also extremely important in reconstructing buildings that have been destroyed; for example, it was used in the reconstruction of the Frauenkirche in Dresden.

Subjects
The variety of architectural subjects is almost infinite. It ranges from the strange and exotic to the very familiar, from ancient to modern, from individual structures to entire complexes. Typical subjects include

houses and offices, stately homes, churches, bridges, industrial buildings, warehouses, railway stations, ports, theatres, and whole districts, towns and cities. Model photographs are an essential component of the design and planning process, and the progress of onsite construction can be documented in pictures.

Once work is complete, the new building is photographed, and it does not stop there: the structure may subsequently undergo renovation, redevelopment or expansion, or be damaged by fire or other disasters, and each time it may need to be photographed again.

Photographic technology
Apart from a camera, the technology required to do justice to architectural subjects includes lenses which allow distortion-free photography of any size of building from a non-central viewpoint, and from any distance or height.

WHAT MAKES A GOOD ARCHITECTURAL PHOTOGRAPH

Many writers have tried to pigeonhole the different types of architectural photography. But these attempts are rarely successful, and the only truly meaningful way of categorising them is by the purpose for which they are taken.

It is also impossible to make dogmatic statements about what makes some architectural photographs good and others bad – again, this depends on their intended purpose, because different criteria of quality apply in each case. For example, a picture taken purely as a documentary record is unlikely to be regarded as an original work of art. Likewise, if it is used to advertise a building for sale or rental, the primary aim will be not so much portraying it realistically as showing it in a good light.

Personal architectural photography
Most architectural photos are personal: holiday photos of villas in Mallorca, hotels in the Caribbean, and buildings seen along the way, or images documenting renovations and extensions to the photographer's own home. Here, the main yardstick of quality is that the photographer likes them. The pictures themselves are of secondary importance, and what matters is the memories they evoke.

Functional photography
Many architectural photos are taken for corporate image and travel brochures, real estate agents' websites and similar purposes. These must be of high quality, but many people will accept compromises to save time and money. For example, a photographer taking pictures for a travel brochure and working to a carefully arranged schedule may be forced to take pictures when the sun is shining from the wrong angle or when the light and weather are less than ideal. Or they may use a small-format camera without lenses that correct perspective.

Reference photography
Architects, urban planners and construction engineers need visual records of their projects. If the buildings involved are particularly spectacular and expensive, the client and photographer will work closely together to ensure that they are captured in uncompromisingly high-quality photographs.

The main challenge with reference photographs is showing reality in a neutral, objective way. But even here, the point is not simply to take a picture of the building: before the photographer presses the shutter, he or she must think about the intended effect of the architecture and find ways of emphasising it, so that it makes a statement about the client and the architect, their view of society, and how they want people to perceive their creation. That said, reference images are not there to fulfil the photographer's artistic ambitions.

Magazine photography
News and arts magazines are another major source of work for the architectural photographer. Unlike reference photographs, these pictures need not be faithful in every detail and photographed to scale, but they must have style and feeling, and lighting and composition are extremely important. They give the photographer a certain amount of leeway in terms of creativity and subjectivity, but they must still be depictions of reality.

Artistic architectural photography
Architectural photographs may also be taken for artistic purposes. They are primarily a form of creative expression, and may make statements quite different from those intended by the architect. The buildings are often simply the photographer's raw material, and the pictures are likely to end up in galleries and on the walls of homes and offices.

Here, the main rule is that there are no rules. The usual criteria of quality and objectivity no longer apply, and the subjective gaze is all that matters. Distortion, blurred movement, converging verticals, grainy images, false colours: anything goes. The same applies to equipment: art photos can be taken just as easily with a cheap instant picture camera as with an expensive view camera.

The standards of quality for art photography are different again. It must get noticed, spark debate, be valued by the public and fetch a high price, and these effects can be obtained only with original images of unusual subjects – or even familiar subjects shown in unusual ways.

Art photography is not even necessarily beautiful: it can be good because it provokes, angers or shocks. Its originality may lie in breaking the rules of good composition – but they cannot be subverted without knowing them in the first place. In music, for example, knowing the theory of harmony does not make you a good composer, and yet there are probably very few successful composers who are not familiar with it.

WHO THIS BOOK IS AIMED AT

This manual is written for people who take pictures of architecture, whether for simple factual reference, publication in glossy lifestyle magazines, sale in art galleries, or just for personal enjoyment. Whether you are an experienced photographer, student, trainee or assistant using a professional tilt-and-shift view camera, or even an ambitious amateur with a compact or small-format fixed-lens camera taking holiday pictures for the family photo album, the same principles apply.

The book tells you how to take better photographs even with limited time and resources, and how to post-edit them to achieve the desired result. It also describes how to use framing, composition, lighting and editing to convey the essence of a building. The best architectural photos do not just happen: they are the fruit of technical and artistic expertise, and careful planning and preparation.

HOW THIS BOOK IS STRUCTURED

The chapter on the optical principles of photography defines the fundamental concepts used when taking architectural photographs with a view camera, such as image circles, stitching, shifting, swinging, and tilting. It also describes how to use the Scheimpflug principle to correct perspective and adjust depth of field.

The next chapter covers the various tools available to architectural photographers, including the advantages and limitations of small-, medium- and large-format and view cameras, fixed and tilt-shift lenses, and analogue and digital backs, with particular reference to taking pictures of buildings.

The chapter that follows puts into practice the principles discussed in the two previous ones. It discusses indoor and outdoor lighting, the effects of weather, time of day and season on the mood of a photograph, and how to take pictures in twilight and at night.
The chapter on composition describes how camera position, distance, angle, focal length and aperture can be used to ensure that the foreground, mid-ground and background are correctly framed and focused. And no book on architecture would be complete without a discussion of lines and the Golden Ratio.

The next chapter deals with the editing process, from digitising analogue pictures to adding the finishing touches, and shows how digital processing can be used to alter the message and effect of the image.

The importance of colour control is often underrated, but professional photographers should be experts in

→ The Linhof Technika 70 studio camera, with a format of up to 6 × 9 centimetres, was produced from 1962 to 1979.

→ This 9 × 12-centimetre plate camera was manufactured by Glunz, of Hanover, around 1925.

this subject, with the ability to calibrate all the hardware involved in the production process and ensure that colour values such as density, temperature and saturation are exactly right.

The next chapter looks at a variety of subjects closely connected with architectural photography: photo composing, artificial worlds, model photography, and photogrammetry, the science of taking measurements from photographs.

The chapter on equipment guides you through the jungle of camera types, image formats, and accessories. Specialist digital cameras are changing very fast, and likely to continue doing so. Good digital backs still cost a small fortune, and second-hand analogue hardware can often be a better buy.

How are the technology and practice of architectural photography likely to develop over the coming years, and what are the prospects for someone considering it as a career? The final chapter looks at ways in to the profession, taking the first steps towards freelancing, and working both with traditional photo agencies and the new low-priced, royalty-free microstock websites.

Chapter 1
The history of architectural photography

Florian Meuser

16 Early technology
23 The beginnings of architectural photography
26 Pictorialism
34 Straight photography
37 *Neue Sachlichkeit*
45 The postwar period

→ The world's oldest surviving architectural photograph, by Joseph Nicéphore Nièpce, shows his country estate in Burgundy. It is believed to date from 1827, and was rediscovered in 1952.

The world's first permanent photograph was a roofscape taken in France over 180 years ago. Made using a homemade camera obscura and with an exposure of several hours, it was also the first architectural photograph. Ever since then the histories of architecture and photography, as both science and art, have been closely interwoven.

This introduction describes the main milestones in this area of photography, and the interdependence between the two fields. A knowledge of the beginnings of photographic technology in the 19th century, and the different ways in which cities and architecture were portrayed in the decades that followed, is hugely important in any assessment of architectural photography. Only by looking to the past can we understand and assess contemporary trends in their historical context.

Architectural photography has always had to tread a delicate balance between factual documentation and artistic freedom. Today, the seemingly limitless possibilities of digital technology have given us a whole new photographic perspective on 21st-century architecture and design. Architecture is better placed than ever before to stimulate public interest in, and understanding of, the built environment.

Unless we are fortunate enough to see it for ourselves, most of us learn about new architecture from words and pictures. The way in which we perceive it therefore depends to a significant extent on its interpretation by the photographer, who is also influential in explaining how the finished building reflects (or in some cases contradicts) the architect's artistic intentions. Photography can force us to look at things in completely different ways, which is why it has such an important status in architectural criticism. It will never replace the reality we perceive with our own eyes, because it reduces three-dimensional objects to two-dimensional likenesses, losing important information in the process. But it can also create greater scope for interpretation or, as the architect Bernhard Tschumi put it, "a longing for something that goes beyond glossy illustrations, a longing for architecture".

→ Historical drawing of a camera obscura

(I.) — EARLY TECHNOLOGY

(I.1) — THE CAMERA OBSCURA

The invention of the camera obscura marked the beginning of modern photography. It consists essentially of a dark box which light rays enter through a lens, forming an inverted image of the subject on the opposite side of the lens. This apparatus, whose principles still govern almost every area of photography, was widespread in the early 19th century, serving as a scientific instrument and a drawing aid for travelling artists. But it actually dates back to ancient times, when it consisted of a room about the height of a man, enclosed on all sides and with a hole in one wall which diffracted the incoming light and created an image of the outside world on the opposite wall.

The camera obscura was first mentioned in the fourth century BC, when Aristotle used it to observe solar and lunar eclipses. It is also referred to in the journals of Leonardo da Vinci, which remained unpublished and unknown for a long period.

Daniele Barbaro was the first to use a lens to improve the focus of the image and turn the camera obscura into an optical instrument used in Renaissance art and experiments with perspective.

But viewers still had to enter a room to view the projected image, and the device did not become portable until the 17th century. The first picture of one, showing a box only 30 to 40 centimetres high, was published in 1686 in Johann Zahn's book *Oculus artificialis*. It has a lens in a metal frame, with a diagonal mirror inside the box creating a realistic picture on the horizontal plane. Once regarded as a magic device used to conjure apparitions, by the 17th and 18th centuries it was a practical tool used by scientists and painters, but it still could not record images using a permanent medium.

The invention of photography is often described as a historic inevitability resulting from advances in optics and chemistry. In fact, some 200 years were to elapse between the invention of the portable camera obscura and the rise of photography.

The connections between the two were little understood, and even in 1800, mankind's knowledge of chemistry was based on a large number of individual observations rather than any overarching methodology. Although Albertus Magnus had noticed as early as the 13th century that silver salts were sensitive to light, this did not become widely known until 1727, in a paper by a German doctor, Johann Heinrich Schulze.[1]

→ Original drawings made by Bernardo Bellotto using a camera obscura.

→ This painting by Bellotto was produced with the help of a camera obscura. It shows the Neumarkt in Dresden.

17 CHAPTER 1: **THE HISTORY OF ARCHITECTURAL PHOTOGRAPHY**

→ The first daguerreotype shows the Boulevard du Temple in Paris. The process was invented by Louis Daguerre in 1837; he and Joseph Nicéphore Nièpce had been working on new image-making techniques since 1829. The French government bought the patent and then made it freely available to the world.

The first attempts at photography were made by an Englishman, Thomas Wedgwood who, in 1802, published *An Account of a Method of Copying Paintings upon Glass*, with Humphry Davy. He copied landscapes and other drawings onto glass by placing them on paper or white leather soaked in silver nitrate and exposing them to daylight. The copies had to be stored in darkness because the silver salts were still light-sensitive and there was no way of fixing them. Attempts to use this method with the camera obscura were unsuccessful, but these experiments were the first step in the slowly evolving science of photography. None of its inventors could ever have imagined the uses to which it would one day be put.

In 1819, the British scientist Sir John Herschel discovered sodium thiosulphate and its ability to dissolve silver chloride. Twenty years later, he realised its applications in photography, and his friend William Henry Fox Talbot demonstrated a simple way of fixing the silver which had turned black in the light by eliminating the remainder of the salts. This method meant that photography was finally possible.

(1.2) —— HELIOGRAPHY

In 1816, Joseph Nicéphore Nièpce (1765–1833), a French officer in Napoleon's army, caused a stir with a technique he called heliography (sun writing). His experiments had two aims.

Firstly, Nièpce wanted to find a way of reproducing existing images, which he saw as a potentially lucrative source of income. He placed engravings, oiled to make them transparent, on surface coated with light-sensitive bitumen. The exposed parts of the image hardened, and the unexposed parts, corresponding to the lines of the original, remained soluble in lavender oil and turpentine. These were then engraved in an acid bath.

Nièpce was also seeking a way of producing images direct from nature in the camera obscura and reproducing these using engraving. He began doing this in 1816, and although his initial attempts with silver chloride on paper were unsuccessful, further experiments using paper, stone and metal and Guayaki resin produced acceptable results. Hydrogen, carbon and acid vapour could be injected into the camera obscura to accelerate the chemical development process.

Nièpce's famous photograph *Maison du Gras* was taken in 1827 on his estate at Le Gras in Burgundy, using an asphalt-coated tin plate. It shows the blurry outlines of the rooftops outside the window of his studio.

He chose the subject for practical reasons: since the technique required several hours' exposure, architecture and landscapes became popular subjects. Walter Benjamin wrote in his history of photography: "The process itself determined the choice of subject, which was no momentary snapshot, but a deep involvement … Everything about these early pictures was made to last."[2]

Nièpce's picture is flat, static and slightly unreal. Because it required eight hours of exposure, the course of the sun created an unnatural distribution of light and shade which is particularly apparent on the roofs.

This unique piece is the oldest surviving photograph. It was discovered by the photographer and photohistorian Helmut Gernsheim in 1952 and donated as part of his collection to the University of Texas at Austin. The picture documents the birth not only of photography, but also of architectural photography.

(1.3) —— THE DAGUERREOTYPE

In 1839 and 1840, three men made major contributions to the development of photographic techniques, with varying degrees of success: Louis Jacques Mandé Daguerre (1787–1851), William Henry Fox Talbot (1800–1877), and Hippolyte Bayard (1801–1887).

Joseph Nicéphore Nièpce had died in 1833, leaving his business partner, Daguerre, with much to thank him for. While Nièpce's first photographs had been elaborately produced one-off creations, Daguerre created a technology that went one step further, using a light-sensitive silver iodide coating on copper plates to create daguerreotypes. Produced in the camera obscura, they took a matter of minutes to create latent negative images, which were then developed with toxic mercury vapour and fixed with sodium thiosulphate. The pictures were one-off mirror images, and could only be viewed from an angle, as the white amalgam meant that all that was visible from the front was a reflective surface.

The daguerrotype was presented to the public at the Institut de France on 19 August 1839, having been explained to and discussed by the members of French Academy of Sciences on 7 January of the same year.

After a multilingual publication on the first patent in photographic history, the technique aroused great excitement throughout the land, and became accepted as a reliable photographic process. One of the few people to have seen a daguerreotype before the public presentation was the American painter and physicist Samuel Finley Breese Morse, inventor of the electromagnetic telegraph, who commented: "The exquisite minuteness of the delineation cannot be conceived. No painting or engraving ever approached it."

In the months that followed, further improvements were made to the daguerreotype technique. Fifteen made by Daguerre himself in 1839 have survived, mostly depicting Paris scenes.

One of his best-known daguerreotypes is the view of the Boulevard du Temple in Paris, now in the Münchner Stadtmuseum. Its sharpness was both revolutionary and unprecedented, and changed society's perceptions of the details of reality, which no art form had ever depicted with such precision.

(1.4) —— THE CALOTYPE

At the same time, important developments were occurring in England. The invention of the calotype is ascribed to the mathematician and Egyptologist William Henry Fox Talbot, and the technique was also known as the talbotype. It was the first negative-positive process, so, unlike the daguerreotype, could be used to make multiple copies of a single image.

Fox Talbot's technique involved placing partly translucent objects of intricate detail on light-sensitive silver paper, and exposing them to the sun for several minutes. The exposed parts darkened, while the unexposed areas remained white with blurred outlines.

He also invented a process whereby the paper negative was coated in wax to make it transparent and then re-exposed to convert it into a positive image. This was not very sharp or detailed, but the method paved the way for photographic reproduction. The earliest surviving calotype, showing a latticed window, dates from 1835 and is also the world's first negative.

While daguerreotypes were exceptionally sharp and brilliant, they were not suitable for reproduction and could not be published in books. The calotype was the future of photography, and the daguerreotype suffered an inexorable decline. The development of the calotype expanded the many uses of photography as an important means of documenting architecture.

(1.5) —— THE COLLODION PROCESS

Changes in the process of making photographs are not simply technical innovations: they directly affect the content and meaning of the image. The rise of the coated glass plate radically changed the nature of photography and the way in which people viewed reality. While techniques such as the heliograph, daguerreotype and calotype were the most important, many others were introduced. Although photographers showed an interest in them, they failed to achieve commercial distribution because they required expensive equipment. The calotype had clear advantages over the daguerreotype, but a new technique was needed to simplify and speed up the negative-positive process.

In 1849 an Englishman, Frederick Scott Archer (1813–1857), began developing a process using light-sensitive glass plates. He applied collodion, a mixture of ether and nitrocellulose dissolved in alcohol (also known as guncotton) to a glass plate, sensitised this using a silver nitrate bath and exposed the plate while its surface was still damp. This had the advantage of requiring only a one-second exposure, being reproducible, and offering greater detail than the calotype.

But photography was still an elaborate process. The exposed glass plates had to be developed immediately because of the light-sensitive collodion, so architectural and landscape photographers had to travel with their own mobile laboratories, including tents and darkrooms, until the dry plate was invented in 1871. Despite these problems, "the collodion process remained the leading photographic technique for several decades, opening up whole new aesthetic possibilities"[3].

(1.6) —— STEREOSCOPE

In 1838, the English physicist Charles Wheatstone introduced an apparatus which combined two different images of the same subject to create the illusion of depth. The stereoscope is based on the principle of binocular eyesight: each eye gives a different picture of the subject because of its position, and the brain combines these into a single three-dimensional image.

This new technique brought further dramatic changes to photographers' and viewers' perceptions of reality. During the late 1800s and early 1900s, when photography was enjoying increasing popularity, no middle-class drawing room was complete without a stereoscope, and even today photographers draw inspiration from this long-since outdated technique: Thomas Ruff used it in his 1995 double photograph of the South Bronx, presenting the two images side by side rather than combining them in the stereoscope, with the bird's-eye perspective rendering the transformation into three dimensions unnecessary. Ruff puts stereoscopy in a new light by grafting an artistic component onto its documentary roots.

→ The Kukeldash madrasah in Tashkent, pictured at some time between 1865 and 1872 by the Russian photographer N. V. Bogayevsky during a tour of Central Asia. His were the first photographs of Turkestan, which had recently been occupied by the Russians.

→ Joseph Paxton's Crystal Palace, photographed by Philip Henry Delamotte in 1852.

(2.) THE BEGINNINGS OF ARCHITECTURAL PHOTOGRAPHY

Because buildings were immobile and photography still required long exposure times, architecture and public spaces became an increasing focus for photographers from the mid-19th century onwards. Although the new medium involved complicated techniques and bulky equipment, it had now at least become portable. People could experience buildings and places which they would otherwise be unlikely to see for themselves, and could even compare multiple places simultaneously.

"In formal terms, 19th-century architectural photographs were an extension of 18th-century vedute paintings and prints, whose compositions and styles they took as their example."[4] Nineteenth-century national monuments, temples and other sacred buildings were the most popular subjects, with photographs being added to the archives in growing numbers.

(2.1) TRAVEL PHOTOGRAPHY

Shortly after the public launch of the daguerreotype, the photographer Emile-Jean-Horace Vernet and his student Frédéric Goupil-Fesquet became the first commissioned travel photographers, journeying to North Africa for a publisher in Paris.

The pair started in Egypt, where they took what was probably the first photograph of the pyramids, and continued to Palestine and Lebanon. Their photographs of cultural monuments were published in France in an album of engravings entitled *Excursions Daguerriennes*. It was described as "the first major commission in photographic history"[5].

Probably the best-known excursion by this first generation of photographers was undertaken by Maxime Du Camp (1822–1894), who travelled to the Orient with Gustave Flaubert in November 1849, described thirty years later in Du Camp's book *Souvenirs Littéraires*.

Du Camp's tour followed in the footsteps of earlier travellers whose drawings and writings had created a mythical view of Egypt in the public mind. But in his case, photography replaced imagination with reality.

These early photographs "heralded a future alliance between photographic journeys of discovery and a steadily growing market for pictures of the remote and exotic – although it would be a while before new technology gradually made travel photography more practicable"[6].

Between 1850 and 1860, following the discovery of the calotype, more and more photographers travelled abroad. It was now possible to reproduce and distribute their pictures, even though the wet collodion process meant that they still had to take mobile darkrooms and other heavy equipment with them.

Photography was fast becoming the principal means of recording the world's historic and archaeological heritage. Large numbers of travel guides, including the famous Baedeker series, were published. "These detailed general routes, important sites, and instructions on where to stay, what to eat, and how to deal with the natives."[7] The guidebooks paved the way for modern tourism, in which photography played an important part.

As the public's interests changed, there was increased demand for illustrated books on foreign architecture. In the introduction to his album *Egypt and Palestine Photographed and Described* (1858–1860), the English photographer Francis Frith (1822–1898) wrote that he wanted to use photography to provide reliable descriptions for those who could not afford the luxury of long-distance travel. He began his own tour of Egypt in 1856, and visited the Middle East in the years that followed. Despite significant problems transporting large amounts of equipment, he brought home an extraordinary treasure trove of photographs. In his 1876 catalogue *Universal Series*, he published some 4,000 mostly architectural images arranged by country and region, which proved a huge success and helped to foster a new view of architecture as a part of the world's cultural heritage.

Frith published an article on photography in *The Journal*, describing the secret of his business success. "We have often found that we notice more details in these realistic pictures than in the subjects themselves. It is easier quietly to contemplate a picture on paper than to be in the presence of the subject, overwhelmed by sensory impressions, uncertainty and excitement, if the subject is of great or unusual interest."[8] The endless succession of personal and professional photographs taken in Egypt and the Middle East from 1839 onwards made these cultural monuments easily accessible for the first time. "Architecture became collectable"[9].

(2.2) DOCUMENTARY PHOTOGRAPHY

The large number of architectural photographs taken in the mid-19th century established photography as an applied art, both in terms of style and technique. Likewise, the popularity of travel photographs led to an increased interest in documentary

September 9, 1887

July 10, 1888

October 14, 1888

December 26, 1888

→ These pictures of the construction of the Eiffel Tower are part of a series of photographs taken at the same location, which Louis-Émile Durandelle and Albert Chevojon used to document the assembly of the Eiffel Tower between 10 August 1887 and 12 March 1889.

photography which gave a true and factual picture of the world, without the artistic ambitions of some photographers.

Two years after the first Great Exhibition in London's Hyde Park in 1851, the English photographer Philip Henry Delamotte (1820–1889) began producing the first comprehensive architectural reportage. He documented the reconstruction in Sydenham of the spectacular Crystal Palace, originally built by Joseph Paxton for the 1851 Great Exhibition and subsequently dismantled. This was the first building to have an exposed glass, wood and iron structure, and used the biggest panes of glass capable of being produced at the time.

The building was constructed entirely of standard mass-produced components, and was one of the first masterpieces of the fast-growing engineering industry. It spawned many imitators, and by the beginning of the 20th century, no doubt thanks partly to Delamotte's series of photographs, it was regarded as a pioneering example of Modernism.

"Philip Henry Delamotte's album was the basis of a new style: it revolutionized architectural photography and shows that people had already realised that the purpose of such a building was not to enclose a space, but to open it up to the world. The famous glass walls, which showed a new appreciation of light as a construction material, gave the Crystal Palace the grace and transparency which its name implied. The structure of the walls reduced the building's overall weight, a characteristic which would soon become widespread throughout architecture."[10]

(2.3) — AERIAL PHOTOGRAPHY

It is very noticeable that until the end of the 19th century, buildings were always photographed in strictly geometrical fashion. "Until its dramatic rise after the first world war, architectural photography was plodding and static. These pictures used central perspective and strict symmetry, and buildings were simply modelled using light. The photographs had almost no personal style."[11] The limitations of cameras were a particular problem with architectural photography, because they created a high degree of distortion and were unable to take wide-angle images, and the development process was very involved. But the visual complexity of architecture spurred photographers to find new perspectives. The first 150-degree panoramic views were taken in 1845, and in 1858 Félix Tournachon Nadar shot the first aerial views from a hot air balloon, literally showing the built environment from a completely new angle.

In his writings, Nadar dwelt at length on the way in which aerial photography transformed the real world into an abstraction. "The fields are like an irregular chessboard, or a brightly coloured patchwork quilt patiently sewn together by a housewife... Everything is exquisitely attractive and clean, no slagheaps, not even a speck of dust. It distances one from everything that is ugly."[12] In the years that followed, balloon photography was increasingly used by cartographers for surveying, and by the military for less peaceful purposes.

(2.4) — SITE DOCUMENTATION

The ability to combine glass and iron allowed 19th-century architects to adopt a whole new direction. The Crystal Palace in Sydenham was the precursor of many new glass buildings, such as the Galleria Vittorio Emanuele in Milan, and also influenced the architecture of greenhouses and botanical gardens, and libraries such as Henri Labrouste's iron-framed Bibliothèque Ste.-Geneviève in Paris. The first skyscrapers and giant exhibition halls were being built in Chicago, and at the height of the industrial revolution the Bisson brothers took an important series of photographs of the Paris universal exhibitions of 1855 and 1867. The pictures stood at the frontiers of architecture, sculpture and mass production, their choice of subject matter itself breaking with the conventions of traditional formalism.

The fourth Paris universal exhibition of 1889 was the star-studded highlight of a technology revolution, providing a chance for engineers such as Gustave Eiffel to display the advances made by their profession: the old Galerie des Machines at the 1855 event, the huge exhibition gallery of 1867, and the two large transepts of the new Galerie des Machines in the same year. This culminated with the construction of the Eiffel Tower, built as the entrance arch for the 1889 exhibition.

The tower's complex four-legged steel construction inspired many important works of experimental photography, and helped to create a new aesthetic sensitivity. Gustave Eiffel commissioned the photographers Louis-Emile Durandelle and Albert Chevojon to produce two series of pictures, entitled *Travaux de construction de la tour Eiffel*, showing the gradual progression from the foundations to the assembly of the firework launching stand for the dedication ceremony.

The photographs focused on the complex interplay of form, space and perspective between the vertical, horizontal and diagonal members. "When the tower was finally completed, the photographer had a new perspective on the frontals, curves, lattices, connectors, girders and stanchions. These structural details were the components of a new abstract rhetoric of mathematical beauty which had never been seen before, because no previous art form was capable of helping people to understand such images."[13]

Early photographs of other steel constructions, such as bridges and the Statue of Liberty, show that photography was creating a new understanding of building structure, and was fast becoming the most important medium of architectural representation. The photographs of Auguste-Hippolyte Collard became a symbol of the complex relationship between man and his greatest technological achievements.

A new era began in engineering and architecture, where the precision of photography increasingly complemented drawings as a form of documentation. The 19th-century photographer Edouard Loydreau described it as a "true and rigorous brush which can very rapidly reproduce any object in nature", adding: "This level of detail will never be achieved by the patience, dedication and talent of a draftsman."[14]

Photographers regarded their art more as a way of conveying information than of expressing themselves as individuals, and their compositions were largely central and symmetrical perspectives of whole buildings rather than details. "These elements made architectural photography perfectly transparent, so that it became purely a tool of documentation ... Just as a drawing attempted precisely to reproduce the three-dimensional subject by using shade and semi-shade, so photography also sought an exact definition of light and shade."[15]

(3.) — **PICTORIALISM**

In the late 19th century, photography shifted its perspective again, questioning the significance, legitimacy and purpose of the image in an effort to contribute to artistic debate. The rise of Impressionism and naturalism encouraged a style widely described as pictorialism, emphasising optical and painterly questions rather than photography. The artistic and aesthetic qualities of the image, and its effect on human emotions, became more important than its subject matter.

"One key aspect of the pictorialist movement was the autonomy of the artwork as an object. Given that a photograph is normally reproducible, and by 1900 photomechanical printing was no longer problematic, it was vitally important for the art photographer to maintain the assumption that his copies were in fact originals. This led to the belief that the created image was unique, that technology could be used to manipulate it, and that its deeper meaning could not be understood until its physical beauty was appreciated."[16]

Gradually, the production of the image assumed a greater importance than that of recording a situation or event; it was about transforming often familiar objects into a new form of two-dimensional visual art. At the same time, the public interest shifted away from the new technology of photography and towards painting, which acquired a much greater cultural status as a result.

Some criticised the camera's detailed portrayal of reality as excessive, leaving no room for artistry, and photographers were forced to come up with new printing and processing techniques which would turn photography into a respected, high-art medium.

(3.1) — NEW TECHNOLOGY

(3.1.1) — Dry plates and focal-plane shutters

An important innovation was the dry plate, invented in 1871. This meant that photographers no longer had to develop their exposed negatives on the spot, turned a manual task into a mass-production process, and made photographic equipment lighter and portable.

The focal-plane shutter was another groundbreaking invention. It made exposure times much shorter, so that street life became an increasingly popular photographic subject: in the age of pictorialism, purely architectural photography was of less interest than naturalistic images of people in harmony with nature and the built environment.

(3.1.2) — The gum bichromate process

Art photographers experimented with new ways of artificially depicting tone and contrast, such as retouching, blurring, and the gum bichromate printing process, invented in 1894 by Robert Demachy (1859–1936). This created distance between the viewer and the photograph, which looked like a charcoal drawing with smudged details. The American photographer Alfred Stieglitz remarked that art photographers now had a medium that could be manipulated in any conceivable number of ways. The gum bichromate technique could be combined with almost any kind of paper, gloss or matte, to reinforce a specific visual statement.

(3.1.3) — The platinum print

Platinum printing, introduced by William Willis in 1878, remained very popular for some thirty years.

→ The Russian photographer Sergei Michailowitch Prokudin-Gorskii (1863–1944) developed a technique, which used colour filters (red/green/blue) which allowed three different shots to be exposed. His negatives were only developed as colour pictures after his death. The pictures show the Palace of the last Emir of Bukhara in Turkestan, under Russian administration. The negatives were created between 1905 and 1915.

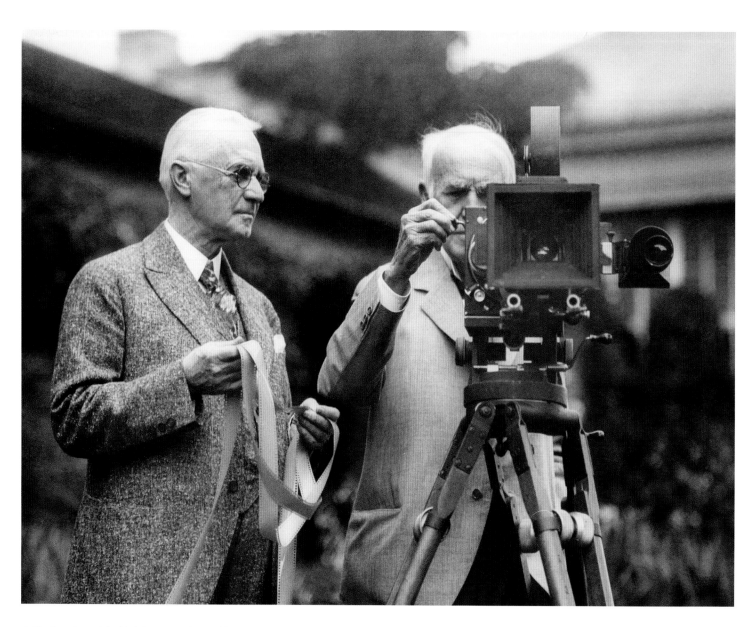

→ The inventors of the Kodak camera, George Eastman and Thomas A. Edison (right) with a film camera in 1928 in the garden of the Eastman house in Rochester, New York.

It created the impression of a washed Indian ink or pencil drawing by preparing the paper with a potassium platinochloride and iron oxalate solution, and then exposing it to diffused light in the normal way. The photograph was developed in potassium or ammonium oxalate, and fixed in an acid bath.

Stieglitz, and the English book dealer Frederick Henry Evans (1852–1943), were enthusiastic advocates of the platinum process, which made it possible to print a wide range of tonal values and create nuances and graining. Evans became well known in the 1890s for his photographs of English cathedrals and French châteaux. The precise detail of the platinum printing process allowed architects to consolidate and refine their knowledge of building as a whole.

The pictorialists used a whole series of other techniques, including the noble process, developed by G.E.H. Rawlins in 1904, and oil printing, which allowed them to finish their photographs in line with their specific objectives.

"Over a long period, a wide range of manipulations came into being, each intended to create a specific effect. They sought to imitate contemporary trends in painting, where style was often more important than substance. In the 1920s, this gave way to a more documentary form of photography which focused on the subject itself."[17]

(3.1.4) — The Kodak camera

In 1888, the American dry plate manufacturer George Eastman designed the first Kodak camera, which used paper negatives to make 100 circular photographs 65 millimetres in diameter. Two years later, the No. 2 Kodak was launched, replacing paper negatives with the first 9×9-centimetre medium-format film roll, followed in the same year by the No. 3 Kodak. This took sixty 9×9 pictures, and was a small, simple 16×9×8-centimetre box with an f9 lens. It had a fixed shutter speed of 1/20 second, a pull string to cock the shutter, and a button release. It had no viewfinder or exposure counter, and cost 25 dollars including one roll of film. When all the pictures had been exposed, the entire camera had to be taken to the developing studio, and the prints were returned to the owner together with a newly loaded camera. "You press the button – we do the rest!" was Kodak's famous slogan.

"The principle of the Kodak system is the separation of the work that any person whomsoever can do in making a photograph, from the work that only an expert can do ... We furnish anybody, man, woman or child, who has sufficient intelligence to point a box straight and press a button, with an instrument which altogether removes from the practice of photography the necessity for exceptional facilities or, in fact, any special knowledge of the art. It can be employed without preliminary study, without a darkroom and without chemicals."[18]

Suddenly, photography became accessible to everyone. Millions of people around the world began photographing their leisure activities, family members and surroundings. Professional photographers, caught unawares by the user-friendliness of this first mass-produced camera, were forced to adopt new techniques to distinguish themselves from amateurs. This quest for novelty was another reason for the development of pictorialism, with its desire to give photography an artistic component.

(3.2) — ART PHOTOGRAPHY

By the late 19th century, photography was moving in two different directions: the first dating back to Daguerre and seeking new ways of portraying contemporary reality, and the second describing itself as art photography, attempting to imitate painting, and enjoying growing popularity. Eventually, most professional photographers and many amateurs opted for the latter.

Photography and painting influenced each other in many important ways. The impact of Impressionist painting was particularly apparent in a photographic movement which flourished around 1900 in London, Paris, Vienna, Hamburg and New York.

In Europe, the pictorialists showed little interest in architectural themes: this was the era of naturalism, in which man and nature were the focus of attention. One example was the English naturalist photographer George Davison (1854–1930), whose images clearly show the influence of Impressionist painting.

In 1891 he declared: "The more photography is a direct experience of nature, the more it influences our aesthetic sensibility. The main characteristic of our eyes is their limited field of vision, and the impossibility of seeing everything in focus at the same time."[19]

Davison's photograph *The Onion Field*, dating from 1890, shows definite impressionistic traits.

"Clearly defined forms are replaced by diffuse tonal values; the layers of landscape have an emotional resonance. A small hamlet lies isolated in a huge field of flowering onion plants, whose glowing, dandelion-like blooms melt together to create a surface as formless as the clouds above. This halftone study of the transitory things of life, emphasized by the smoking chimney and laundry fluttering in the wind, gives the old farmhouses a human dimension in an otherwise abstract landscape."[20]

Photography was still seen as a scientific medium because of its precision, and the influence of painting caused little concern. Some photographers sought to give a painterly quality to architectural photographs whose primary purpose was documentary by including the building's environment. André-Adolphe Eugène Disdéri, who spawned a craze for photographic "cartes de visite" and invented the twin-lens reflex camera, wrote in 1864 that because of its technological basis, photography could not change the relationship between architecture and its surroundings. "But it can still change a view in any way it likes through its choice of viewpoint and distance, thus preserving the effects of perspective which we see in the most distinctive paintings."[21]

(3.3) —— URBAN PHOTOGRAPHY

Many European cities enjoyed an economic boom in the wake of late 19th-century industrialisation, and local authorities sparked social conflict by carrying out extensive redevelopments of decaying city centres where large numbers of poor people lived cheek by jowl.

Many painters and photographers chronicled these events in their own neighbourhoods, in street scenes where, for the first time, humans became the principal subjects and photography became reportage. The Berlin artist Heinrich Zille (1858–1929), who took photographs as the basis for his drawings, carried out a detailed visual survey of the city's working-class districts from 1890 onwards. These naturalistic and undramatic views of old streets, manual workers, and women collecting firewood were intended not as a call to arms against poverty but "to show what the photographer saw: portrait as analytical documentary"[22]. Rather than simply depicting what was on public view, Zille took his camera into courtyards and onto staircases and produced sequences of images that tell a story.

(3.3.1) —— Eugène Atget

While Zille concentrated mainly on sociological studies of Berlin's working-class districts, the French photographer Eugène Atget (1857–1927) documented the architecture of the Paris suburbs. Until 1927, he specialised in the city's intimate early-morning street scenes rather than its great monuments, regarding photography as both a complement to and a basis for contemporary Impressionist painting.

Atget's buildings are always shown in the context of their surroundings, and thus of their time. His distant, almost alienated views of empty streets, backyards, shops, architectural details and roofscapes were particularly popular among the surrealist painters. Atget wanted to document all the districts which had survived Baron Georges-Eugène Haussmann's large-scale redevelopment of 1853 to 1870. His pictures "were taken from eye level, focusing on people strolling by, rather than using a higher viewpoint to gain a more objective view and avoid converging lines. Atget's subjective gaze and individual perception talk to us through his pictures and create an authentic image of the city"[23].

Atget believed that "art has nothing to do with being chosen or gifted, but simply results from experience of working in a particular environment"[24]. He was a part of the Paris milieu, and was able to photograph everyday situations in ways suggesting that something else lay hidden behind them. Because he was so much at home with the everyday, he was able to make things speak or, as Walter Benjamin wrote, "transform them into evidence of a historic process"[25].

"The familiar seems unfamiliar, and his piercing gaze brings the unfamiliar claustrophobically close. In this confusing fragmentation of time, his city scenes are as contemporary today as when he photographed them."[26]

"Here, the intention of the photograph is eclipsed by the effect of the subject it portrays. The buildings are shown without using lighting and perspective for effect. They often look flat and ornamental, almost pattern-like, so despite their documentary nature they are aesthetically attractive to the modern-day viewer. This reevaluation of attitudes towards reality was fundamental to 20th-century photography."[27]

Walter Benjamin believed that these pictures were so expressive because the photographer was personally involved, "not yet spoiled by commercial interests or using accessories to create effects which falsify the essence of architecture"[28].

Eugène Atget was one of the few photographers to attempt factual, documentary depictions of buildings without displaying his contemporaries' tendency towards alienation. He was the most important representative of a new style which lay closer to *Neue Sachlichkeit*, new objectivism, than to the earlier pictorialism. From an art historical point of view, he was a unique photographer who played a major part in the subsequent development of his craft. Most of Atget's extensive archive is now in the Musée Carnavalet and the Bibliothèque de l'Ecole des Beaux-Arts in

→ Photograph of a cobbler's workshop in Berlin by Heinrich Zille from 1900.

→ Heinrich Zille used his photographs of workers' neighborhoods in Berlin as the basis for his later drawings.

→ Photograph of a broken-down Renault soft-top in a courtyard in Rue de Valence in Paris, taken by Eugène Atget in 1922.

Paris, and the Museum of Modern Art in New York. His American friend, the surrealist painter Berenice Abbott (1898–1991), who ended up in the artists' district of Montparnasse, was an enthusiastic photograph collector before she began taking pictures herself. After Atget's death in 1927, she marketed his work and developed her own style, influenced by his.

(3.4) —— THE NEW PICTORIALISM

A new generation of pictorialists grew up at the beginning of the 20th century. Contrary to the dominant trend whereby photographers deliberately manipulated images to give them the artistic value of an original painting, some returned to a less distancing and more factual portrayal of reality. The author Henry McBride noted in a 1913 article in the *New York Sun*: "Photography can state concrete facts expressively without manipulating the negative or arranging objects in any special way."

The new pictorialism spread more quickly in some countries than others, partly due to the effects of the first world war and the controversy caused by some exhibitions. Generally speaking, though, it largely abandoned the fundamental rule of pictorialism that the subject be expressive and unique.

In formal terms, pictorialism developed along similar lines to painting, sculpture and poetry between 1890 and 1920: "Art generally withdrew from the realms of the eternal verities and moved closer to the natural sciences, technology and the realities of urban living."[29]

(3.4.1) —— Japonisme

Japonisme exerted an important influence on late pictorialist composition, combining the decorative forms of old Japan with the linearity of contemporary architecture. It characterised by its stark simplification, emphasis on diagonals, objects left partly out of the frame, carefully composed foregrounds, silhouette-like figures and impression of depth.

Alfred Stieglitz and Edward Steichen were famous for their consistent use of aspects of this style, which made its way from Japan to North America in the form of original prints, paintings and publications.

(3.4.2) —— Skyscraper architecture

Around 1920, the focus of pictorialism shifted from rural, symbolic subjects to big cities, new technology and modern architecture. Urban life and architecture once again became the most popular subjects, leaving symbolism a spent force.

The first skyscrapers were built in New York and Chicago, with steelframe technology and the invention of the elevator sparking a competition to construct the world's highest building, a symbol of modernity and progress. People were fascinated and overwhelmed by the upward growth of cities, and ready for a new style of architecture which would project American prosperity to an international audience.

The varied perceptions of architecture at this time can be seen in the work of three photographers regarded as pioneers of the new avant garde: Alfred Stieglitz, Edward Steichen and Alvin Langdon Coburn.

In the space of ten years, all three photographed the Flatiron Building in New York, built by the US architect Daniel Hudson Burnham. When completed in 1902, it was the world's highest building, and became a popular subject for professional and amateur photographers. Located at the busy intersection of Broadway and Fifth Avenue, it became a hub of the city's social and commercial life.

Described at the time as "the most famous thing in New York", the Flatiron Building attracted "more attention than all the other new buildings put together"[30]. With its huge steel skeleton, it is still one of New York's most important structures.

Alfred Stieglitz (1864–1946) photographed the wedge-shaped skyscraper in 1903, on a snowy winter's day shortly after it was completed. The picture makes it look like a big ship with its bows dug in to the earth. "Although it is a part of the city, the building behind the white veil has something mysterious about it", writes Peter C. Bunnell. "This symbol of industry and trade symbolises the relationship between human experience and the fabric of the city."[31]

Edward Steichen (1879–1973) photographed the building in 1905 from a completely different perspective. The picture is dramatic and impressionistic, taken in the shimmering light of early morning, with a strong foreground of pedestrians and coaches silhouetted against the rain-soaked streets.

The majestic building dominates the background of the picture. The top of the structure has been left out of the frame, adding drama to the scene and giving it a two-dimensional feel. There is no clearer example of modern composition in the field of architectural photography, and the work combines a contemporary metropolitan idiom with a hint of the Japanese.

Alvin Langdon Coburn (1882–1966) took late pictorialism one step further with his 1912 picture of the Flatiron Building as a ship moving to the echo of passers-by and branches waving in the wind. The restless, confused blurriness of the image is totally urban, and its theme would occupy photographers for a long time to come as city architecture grew in importance.

Later, Coburn went beyond the basic ideas of pictorialism with a series of cubist, constructivist photographs, parts of which he manipulated by overlapping, in an interpretation of abstract painting. Like Pablo Picasso's pictures, they show signs of a new relationship between art and reality, and this specific form of visual expression was based on a new theory of perception.

"Never has an attempt been made to express things observed not as they are known, but as they are seen, without remembering that we have looked upon them."[32]

(4.) STRAIGHT PHOTOGRAPHY

While the First World War brought suffering and destruction in Europe, and the arts went into hibernation, the commercialisation of photography caused a change of direction in the United States. The aesthetics of form, documentary and technology came to the fore as photography once again became a factual, realistic art form. It had already been recognised by the up-and-coming advertising industry as the medium of the future, and the symbols and products of industrialisation – factories, machines, skyscrapers, automobiles and other consumer goods – became popular photographic themes.

It was believed that photography would stand as an art form in its own right if it could transcend its own physical realism. "It needed to take ordinary, everyday subjects and idealise them historically, symbolically or methodologically."[33]

Photographic realism was redefined on the basis of the American approach to contemporary European art in general, and analytic Cubism in particular. The Mexican artist and head of New York's Modern Art Gallery, Marius de Zayay, made a clear distinction between artistic and "straight" photography, believing that the purpose of the former, as propounded by Edward Steichen, was to attract interest and express feelings.

Straight photography, practised by Alfred Stieglitz and Paul Strand, eliminated both the subject and the system of representation. It was "independent and impersonal experimentation, leading to an understanding of the subject"[34].

Unlike pictorialism's subtle gradations of tone, straight photography was dominated by strong black-and-white contrasts, sharpness and depth, and close-up detail, printed on expensive, glossy platinum or other photographic paper. The reproduction process became simpler, much to the delight of the advertising industry.

(4.1) AMERICAN ARCHITECTURAL PHOTOGRAPHY

(4.1.1) Alfred Stieglitz

Stieglitz was one of the most prominent figures in the American photographic avant-garde of the 1920s. He studied mechanical engineering in Berlin, and worked as a magazine editor and photojournalist in New York before founding the 291 art gallery and the glossy magazine *Camera Work* for the New York Photo Secession group in 1902. This was intended as an international forum for trends in photography, and included articles by professional photographers, detailed descriptions of development processes, and background features. The magazine published 50 quarterly issues between 1903 and 1917.

It has been claimed that Stieglitz, like Coburn, planned to continue manipulating his images in the manner of the pictorialists because, contrary to common practice, he shifted alienation away from the negative and towards the realistic subject. This is apparent in his series *View from the Window*, taken from the 291 gallery, a dense, cubist portrayal of urban architecture half a world away from the elegant façades of Fifth Avenue. The two most important compositional features are the framing and the emphasis on emphasising forms within their context, and these, combined with the tonal contrasts, create an abstract composition which nevertheless offers a realistic and critical view of the metropolis.

(4.1.2) Paul Strand

Shortly before the First World War, Stieglitz met Paul Strand (1890–1976), who also advocated straight photography and joined the Photo Secession group. The last two issues of *Camera Work*, which officially introduced straight photography as a form of artistic expression in the United States, were dedicated to him.

Strand took pleasure in simple subjects, such as down-at-heel suburban streets, telegraph poles and everyday objects, and was also the first to photograph machines and their components. Unlike the art photographers whose pictures created an imaginary intellectual world, Strand found his themes in the raw reality of everyday life. He explains his cubist approach

→ Edward Steichen photographed the Flatiron Building, the first skyscraper in New York, in April 1906 at dusk.

→ Paul Strand's famous photograph *The White Fence* taken in 1917 has a surprising composition.

in the text accompanying the pictures: "Honesty, no less than intensity of vision, is the prerequisite of a living expression. This means a real respect for the thing in front of... the photographer ... This is accomplished without tricks of process or manipulation through the use of straight photographic methods."[35]

Strand produced a number of portrait studies, and a series of pictures carefully framed to take alienation to its limits, so that the viewer must first find the key to understanding them. In his 1916 photograph *The White Fence*, the houses and the garden fence in the foreground are drawn together to create a flat composition. Despite the camera's spatial depth, Strand avoided creating perspective in order to maintain a specific pictorial character.

An even more striking example is his picture Shadows of a Veranda. "So consistent is the alienation from reality, with its black-and-white photography and the jarring use of framing, that it is difficult to reconstruct the original situation."[36] Strand's clear affinity for factual photography harks back to the very first photographs by Daguerre and other 19th-century pioneers.

(4.1.3) —— Charles Sheeler

At this time, Strand was living with Charles Sheeler (1883–1965), who had made a name for himself first as a painter in a style similar to Edward Hopper's, and later with commissioned photographs of architectural details and advertising products. He regarded his pictures like drawings, something very personal created using an impersonal piece of equipment. "Sheeler wanted to show that the foundations of modern art could also be found in nature, and taken to the limits of abstraction."[37]

In 1920, Sheeler and Strand released a six-and-a-half-minute documentary silent film entitled *Manhatta*, showing a series of images of skyscrapers, ships and busy streets in the lower Manhattan financial district. This was the first purely architectural film in history, with the images brought together to make them easier to understand than individual photographs. Its impartial view of the city's architecture provided the basis for further series of New York photographs by the two artists.

In 1914, Strand began taking interior photographs, beginning with his house in Pennsylvania. All twelve pictures in the first series follow the same principle: a single, bright but covered light source, details or household objects bathed in harsh light, and other objects appearing hard edged in the reflected light. Sheeler's compositions did not illuminate the architecture, size and spatial depth of the room, but shed direct light on specific areas, transforming them into relief-like compositions. In his picture *Interior with Stove*, the dark, abstract outlines of the stove dominate the foreground, and the brightly lit surrounding space with its individually identifiable subjects forms the background. The window, for example, is shown not as an architectural detail but as an abstract element of the composition.

One of Sheeler's best-known photoseries is his 1932 triptych *Industry*, showing large, clearly recognizable forms from industrial architecture and mechanical engineering. Careful framing destroys any sense of depth, reducing the pictures to flat graphic images and turning three-dimensional space into a two-dimensional surface. This subjective, interpretive approach to photography is a clear sign of the break between pictorialist and straight photography, in which American photography finally engaged in a direct dialogue with architecture. "Architects and architectural photographers began seeing things with the same eyes."[38]

(4.1.4) —— Ansel Adams

In 1933, Alfred Stieglitz met 31-year-old Ansel Adams (1902–1984). He was hugely impressed by Adams' talent, and three years later devoted an exhibition to him at his New York gallery, An American Place.

While Adams' later photographs had a strong sense of three-dimensionality, his early works were two-dimensional Cubist creations, consisting mainly of portraits, windmills, posters on walls, and factories, with flat, graphic styles similar to Sheeler's strict realism. During this time, Adams and a number of other contemporary photographers formed the f/64 group: as the name implies, they were masters of structure, detail, and wide depth of field.

(5.) —— **NEUE SACHLICHKEIT**

The economic boom of the 1920s opened Germany up to the foreign artistic and cultural influences of the postwar period, and increased the role of cultural mass production. In photography, it quickly adopted the American concept of straight photography and its compositional resources. "Subjects previously regarded as banal, such as factories, industrial products and natural forms, were used as the basis for highly functional industrial designs."[39]

Neue Sachlichkeit, or New Objectivity, was heavily influenced by German and Soviet constructivism, and its preoccupation with technology and construction. It sought to make these ideas a reality using a very wide range of styles with a strong emphasis on photographic focus, viewing objects from above and below, at an angle, in closeup, or in fragmented form.

Photography had become a medium in its own right, no longer simply a way of illustrating information, but the most important way of gaining access to things themselves. Albert Renger-Patzsch, whose work is discussed in a separate chapter, is regarded as the founder and most important proponent of *Neue Sachlichkeit* in Germany.

(5.1) —— NEUES SEHEN

In the United States, the architectural photographers Paul Strand, Charles Sheeler and Alfred Stieglitz were using formal means such as unconventional framing, exaggerated contrast and large flat spaces to maintain the connection between architectural and art photography. In Germany, the Neues Sehen (new way of seeing) movement also served a documentary purpose.

Neues Sehen is "the expression of a very optically oriented view of reality ... The dominance of seeing resulted in increasingly strong visualisation of a reality primarily shaped for visual effect."[40] These photographers aimed to make the perception process visible and use it to create spatial effect, and also to incorporate artistic resources into the equation. In this way, the resources became components of a perception which, as a result of changes in location, extended into the fourth dimension, which in turn could be seen as the subject of the images.

After the First World War, Russian art freed itself from its close dependence on artistic trends in Western Europe. Its response to European Cubism was Suprematism which, even more than Cubism, reduced things to basic geometric forms.

The best-known suprematist photographer was the constructivist painter and graphic artist Alexander Rodtschenko (1891–1956), who made a name with his extreme wide-angle perspectives. His photographic style was influenced by the Russian painter, designer and architect El Lissitzky (1890–1941) who, mainly during his study in Darmstadt, experimented intensively with photomontage and propagated a synthesis of painting and architecture which Rodtschenko transposed into photography.

(5.2) —— NATURE AND ARCHITECTURE

With the growing interest in scientific and technological innovation, photography was increasingly used for scientific purposes. Alongside experiments with directly exposed photograms, this was about using photography not so much to expand visual information as to extend the range of sensory impressions.

One important figure who explored the artistic possibilities of this new trend was Karl Blossfeldt (1865–1932), who was not a professional photographer, but taught sculpture at the Kunstgewerbeschule in Berlin, specialising in models of plants. In 1900 he began using macro photography as a teaching aid, finding unusual and expressive forms in very common flora.

Blossfeldt used close-ups to make natural phenomena visible to the human eye and record them for science, always photographing plants from the same camera position and in small numbers. By rearranging what he saw, he transformed plant details into abstract, architecture-like images. Like Art Nouveau, Blossfeldt regarded natural structures as the archetypes of industrial forms, and incorporated these to impressive effect in his 1928 book *Urformen der Kunst* (Archetypes of Art).

Much the same is true of some 20th- and 21st-century skyscrapers, such as the Jin Mao Tower in Shanghai, designed by the American architects Skidmore, Owings and Merrill (SOM). The third highest building in the world, at 420 metres, its architecture reinterprets scientific phenomena. There are unmistakable parallels between SOM and Blossfeldt, and although there is not necessarily any direct connection between the photographic detail of the 1920s and architecture in the new millennium, photographers and architects have long taken their aesthetic and structural inspiration from such forms.

(5.3) —— THE BAUHAUS

In 1919, Walter Gropius founded a school of applied arts, at the Kunstgewerbeschule in Weimar. Taking its inspiration from the Deutscher Werkbund and Britain's Arts and Crafts movement, the Bauhaus provided teaching in a wide variety of disciplines. It moved to Dessau in 1925.

The Hungarian painter László Moholy-Nagy (1895–1946) taught at the Bauhaus from 1923 to 1928, giving basic courses and managing the metal workshop. In 1925, he expounded his artistic theories in a book published by the Bauhaus entitled *Malerei, Fotografie, Film*. This also includes a summary of various photographic processes which had previously been employed in isolation, and is still used as a manual today by graphic artists in the advertising industry, though it clearly exercised little influence on photographers.

→ This photograph, taken by Paul Strand in 1917, shows a paving stone in New York with the shadow of the steel construction of a bridge.

→ Karl Blossfeldt transformed details of plants into architecture-like images by using strict arrangements. The two photographs on the left were published in 1928 in the volume *Urformen der Kunst* (Archetypes of Art), and the photograph on the lower right in 1932 in *Wundergarten der Natur* (Magic Gardens of Nature).

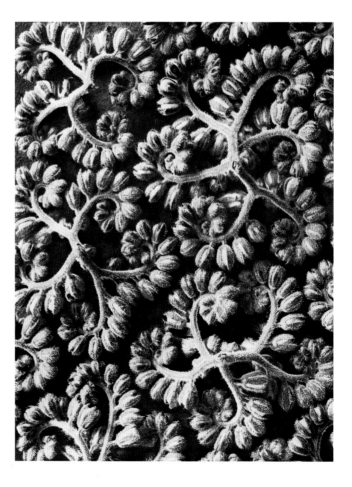

Moholy-Nagy proclaimed: "Painting is a craft, photography a technology." His radical demand that photography replace traditional painting as a medium of visual communication was based on the belief that it was a better expression of the age of technology. He strove to dematerialise reality by ensuring that the material was no longer the main element of his images, and believed that pure light was the ideal way of achieving this fundamental goal.

In his quest for optical laws, Moholy-Nagy reduced the process of taking photographs to his terms. One result was photograms, in which he created forms using only light and which gave him the ability to organise reality optically. He was also enthused by the intangible aspects of glass façades, the lighting of big cities, and the weightless dynamism of modern life.

"Moholy-Nagy set himself the task of studying and using the optical reality of photography and its nature as a phenomenon, in the same way as abstract painting had done in relation to its underlying forms. He believed that photographic phenomena which had previously been regarded as errors, such as converging lines and hard shadows, should be used for compositional purposes, and used very unusual angles to create a completely new repertoire of forms."[41]

The meaning of these photographs lies in the purely optical reproduction of the image, complete with distortion and foreshortening. "Our eyes associate the things we see and our intellectual experience to create a formal and spatial image in our minds."[42]

(5.3.1) —— Bauhaus photography

Until Walter Peterhans was appointed in 1929, there was no photography class at the Bauhaus, though Moholy-Nagy's basic course experimented with this medium a great deal. In 1923, his wife Lucia Moholy (1894–1989) came to the Bauhaus and initially worked with portrait photography; Walter Gropius very much admired her work, and shortly afterwards commissioned her to produce a photographic record of the construction of the Bauhaus in Dessau.

As well as chronicling the progress of the main building, Lucia produced more factual photographs of Bauhaus furniture for advertising purposes, and took detailed photographs of the interiors of Paul Klee and Wassily Kandinsky's houses. Her architectural pictures were simply crafted, their documentary and historic interest rarely transcending the factual, but she also occasionally experimented with composition, often prompted by debates on photography with her husband and his colleagues.

"For example, she photographed the projecting façade of the main Bauhaus building from an extremely low angle, so that the vertical lines of the front and edges of the building tend towards a central vanishing point above the top of the picture. The horizontals create a powerfully diverging angle from the bottom left to the top right-hand corner, counterpointed by the flat white upper left third of the picture. Showing all the audacity of the Neues Sehen movement, this is the only architectural photograph of its kind taken by Lucia Moholy."[43]

Even after Walter Peterhans began teaching his photography class, architectural photography played little part in studies at the Bauhaus, and Lucia Moholy's picture appears to have been a one-off creation. Apart from Erich Mendelsohn and Richard Neutra, few classic modern architects made use of photography as a medium, which is surprising given that Bauhaus theory had so much to say about it. Mendelsohn published a small book of photographs of America in 1926, showing his enthusiasm for Charles Sheeler's straight photography.

In the 1920s, Neutra became one of the first German-speaking architects to emigrate to the United States. He joined the f/64 group, but saw photography simply as a means of preserving personal memories. Most photographs of his buildings were taken later by Julius Shulman (1910–2009), who gained a reputation for carefully staged images of attractive locations in Southern California. Shulman's work still has a great influence on contemporary photographers, and occupies a unique position in the medium's history.

(5.3.2) —— *Neue Sachlichkeit* and its influences

Partly as a result of Richard Neutra's factual depictions of architecture, and their popularisation in the United States by Julius Shulman, a small number of Bauhaus photographers did influence architectural photography on the other side of the Atlantic. Apart from Ezra Stoller who, like Shulman, became a known for his simple black-and-white photographs of American architecture, other young photographers discovered the rural architecture of the Midwest. The strong graphic structure of picket fences, clapboard houses and corrugated iron roofs worked particularly well in black and white.

One of the main protagonists of rural architectural photography in America was Walker Evans (1903–1975), the first photographer to combine architecture with social reportage. In the early 1930s, when there were plans to abolish state subsidies for impoverished farmers, Evans' documentation of their struggle for existence played a major part in maintaining the financial support they received. The publication of the photographs caused a stir nationwide. "Evans' photographic philosophy was very similar to *Neue Sachlichkeit*, and was ideally suited to this project."[44]

Because this new view of reality had become so popular, Evans' photographs could also be used for social and political purposes. His analytical observations of the streets of New York focused on the random, unimportant and unknown. His camera was a tool for gathering and disseminating ideas, with no particular artistic intent.

Evans placed arbitrarily chosen subjects into new contexts, giving them added importance by careful cropping and sequencing in his books, which included *American Photographs* and *Let Us Now Praise Famous Men*.

"His photographs are about surfaces that reveal the true nature of their surroundings. For example, the furniture, household objects and pictures in a room can say more about the inhabitants than if they had actually been included in the picture. He creates as much distance as possible between himself and the subject, and describes anonymity as a precondition for aesthetic freedom."[45]

Walker Evans' attempts to capture in his photographs what Walter Benjamin described as the "visual unconscious" were his first attempt to create a greater awareness of the relationships between everyday objects and their owners. His pioneering work was one of the main reasons for the dramatic rise in the popularity of illustrated books about specific cities and countries, showing humans' dependence on architecture.

(5.4) —— ALBERT RENGER-PATZSCH

The main founder and proponent of *Neue Sachlichkeit* in Germany was Albert Renger-Patzsch (1897–1966). From 1922 onwards, he worked as head of the picture department at the Folkwang-Archiv in Essen, where he worked with macro photographs of natural and man-made objects. These appeared to have been taken out of scientific interest, but he realised that they also had considerable aesthetic value.

Renger-Patzsch's work is characterized by precise perception, surprising subjects, sharp images and an emphasis on detail. Like those of Karl Blossfeldt, his pictures of plants look very similar to botanical illustrations, and show unmistakable parallels with intricate architectural structures.

Both artists regarded architectural forms as rooted in nature. Unlike Blossfeldt, who concentrated exclusively on the artistic documentation of plants, Renger-Patzsch gained his insights from the natural sciences and extended these into the broader environment by taking pictures of landscapes, architecture and technology.

His architectural images are dominated by diagonals and unusual angles, and full of movement, their aesthetics drawing on the representational techniques of documentary photography. "They reflect a positivist striving for objective knowledge, fixing a single moment in a timeless record of the subject, just as any collection of pictures taken for scientific purposes must do."[46]

Renger-Patzsch held that the photographer should actively intervene to ensure that the subject can continue to exist objectively and unchanged in the photograph. The subject of the image was more important than the resources used to depict it, such as alienation and staging, and more important than the photographer's personal reasons for taking the picture. Its role was to serve as a precise document of a building and its history, design, materials and construction.

"The photographic process includes images of the subject, such as an individual building, a type of architecture, or buildings from a particular era. Renger-Patzsch did not simply use the camera to capture the external appearance of the building, for example by panning across the front, but took pictures of interiors, architectural details, and neighbouring or similar buildings, to bring out the connections between the forms and components of architecture."[47]

Many of Renger-Patzsch's photographs contradict his theories and reveal his personal preferences. For example, he often isolated architecture from its urban context using heavy cropping and unusual angled perspectives. But many features remained consistent throughout his work, such as the 3:4 ratio of the sides (regardless of the picture format), and the use of low-contrast greys. "The need for documentary objectivity remained an unachievable ideal even for Renger-Patzsch."[48]

The illustrations in his 1930 book on the brick cathedrals of northern Germany show that this is particularly true of architectural photography. Not one picture shows the entire façade of a building: even where he is placing a church in its urban context, he uses dramatically low angles which distort its proportions. Buttresses are often hidden in shadow, making

→ Photographic course at Bauhaus Dessau
(photograph by Etel Mittag-Fodor)

43   CHAPTER 1: **THE HISTORY OF ARCHITECTURAL PHOTOGRAPHY**

→ The photograph was taken by Walker Evans in 1935 and shows a smallholder's hut, with washing facilities and a kitchen, in Hale County, Alabama.

their exact position unclear, and many of the interior scenes focus on details in an attempt to explore the architect's artistic intentions rather to reproduce them exactly.

(6.) — THE POSTWAR PERIOD

During the Second World War, architectural photographers in Germany were forced to work for newly created propaganda units, documenting buildings and cultural monuments. By the end of the war, with a large proportion of these destroyed and cities razed to the ground, photographs of the destruction, homecoming soldiers and their wives and children were an important way of coming to terms with what had happened. Photographers wanted to preserve the terrors of war for posterity, and gave free rein to their individual creativity and choice of subject matter.

The architectural photography of the time was more stylistically homogeneous. Its main purpose was to document Germany's reconstruction – as having "a strong emphasis on perspective, nearly always in landscape format because there was so little architecture left standing, and with a few people in the foreground to add interest and scale. Colour photographs frequently showed people dressed in red or yellow with a green mid-ground, a brightly coloured building and an ultramarine sky"[49].

Humans were rarely shown interacting with architecture: in most cases they were simply accessories. Some photographs showed cars parked in front of the buildings, particularly when the architect needed to show the connection between the architecture and the traffic – a practice adopted by Le Corbusier in the 1920s. As colour became more widespread, architects insisted that photographs of their work in architectural publications comply with these rules, seeing them as the epitome of technical perfection. The pictures were rarely creative, with the exception of the occasional monographs on architecture or construction, and the photographer's personal involvement was limited to minor differences of framing and angle.

Before-and-after images were very common during the postwar period, showing the same building before the war, destroyed after the conflict, and then reconstructed, and shot from the same position each time. The photographer Karl-Hugo Schmölz (1917–1986) was commissioned by a news agency in Cologne to document the destruction wrought on the city. Rolf Sachsse points out: "The unusual thing about the concept of this album was that it reversed the normal order by showing things getting worse, not better: it focused on the destruction, though this was described as capable of being repaired."[50]

(6.1) — SUBJECTIVE PHOTOGRAPHY

In 1949, a circle of photographers led by Otto Steinert (1915–1978) established the fotoform group, inspired by the Bauhaus of the 1920s and early 1930s. They displayed a collection of highly original photographs at the Cologne *Photokina* exhibition in 1950, featuring strict compositions, strong contrasts and a predilection for structure.

Steinert played an important part in a change of artistic direction in postwar German photography: the rise of subjective photography. In contrast to purely documentary images, he said, this should include "all areas of personal photography, from abstract photograms to the psychological depth and visual impact of reportage".

The group subsequently took part in a series of exhibitions showing their strong personal perspective and clear aesthetic position on the nature and form of photography. This sought to confirm what Sachsse describes as "the creative power of photography ... the only thing capable of transforming a subject into a picture"[51].

Steinert's most famous photograph is the punningly titled *Ein-Fuss-Gänger*, meaning both "one foot walking" and "a pedestrian". Dating from 1950, it is a bird's-eye view of a pavement, with the distorted perspective of the tree and circular metal grille on the left reminiscent of pictures by the Bauhaus photographer Moholy-Nagy, and the pedestrian on the right blurred almost into nonexistence, recognisable only by one foot. This out-of-focus movement and deliberate choice of framing and perspective are so abstract that the picture can be described as an extension of the Neues Sehen of the Bauhaus era.

Two other photographers employed this subjective style of simplified forms and large black and white prints. Robert Häusser (b. 1924) used architecture as the main subject of his haunting images. His 1953 series *Peripherie* shows a tapering, angular building set between railway tracks, with a pond and an area of sand dominating the foreground, and the white sky covering two thirds of the picture. The diffuse light means there is little shadow, and the low angle at which the building is photographed, emphasized by the converging rails, puts the derelict building very much in the context of its surroundings, a deserted industrial wasteland.

Another photograph from 1963 shows a pipeline in a chemical works in Ludwigshafen. The architecture of the factory recedes into the background, rendering it insignificant, while the foreground is dominated by the three amorphous pipes and their distributor valves, the flat white sky and lack of human presence making the pipes even more striking.

This monumentalisation of industrial buildings is typical of Häusser, whose series may have inspired Bernd and Hilla Becher, the first photographers systematically to document industrial buildings in the Ruhrgebiet and other locations in Germany and abroad.

→ This photograph taken by Hugo Schmölz shows the commercial vocational school designed by the architect Dominikus Böhm at Montagsmarktplatz in the Upper Silesian city of Hindenburg/Zabrze.

→ Bernd and Hilla Becher in 1985 at an exhibition in Museum Folkwang in Essen. (photograph by Marga Klingler)

(6.2) —— ARTISTIC DOCUMENTARY PHOTOGRAPHY

Bernd Becher (1931–2007) and his wife Hilla (b. 1934) sparked a renaissance in documentary and object photography during the 1960s. In the late 1950s, they turned against the subjectivity which had dominated photography since the end of the war, and used the camera as a means of documentation.

Their subjects were not elegant stately homes but abandoned and anonymous industrial buildings such as cooling and water towers and factories, and also half-timbered houses.

"The individual photographs are taken with comparability in mind ... In other words they are shot in accordance with fixed rules: at right angles to or diagonally in front of the object, as far away as possible and with the longest possible focal length. This isolates the subject from its surroundings and reduces the distortion caused by foreshortened perspective, diffuse light (usually in the early morning) white sky, muted background tones, fine-grained film and finely graded black-and-white prints."[52]

All of the photographs are very similarly framed, turning the subjects into a series of anonymous sculptures, and the individual images gain in meaning when viewed as a series.

The Bechers' work is based on comparisons of their subjects' outward appearance, which are classified by type in large-format pictures so that they can be viewed side by side. Other series concentrate on individual items of architecture, mostly in the form of eight photographs. The couple made an important contribution to a new awareness of the need for architectural conservation, transmuting historic industrial buildings and even dystopias into objects of beauty, a symbiosis of art and documentation previously achieved only by Eugène Atget's photographs of Paris.

"Eugène Atget's architectural collections, both individually and as an overall concept, deeply impressed the Surrealists in 1920s Paris. The Bechers proved worthy successors, their conceptual strength lying probably not so much in the viewer's relationship with the subject (as in Atget's work), as in the relationship between the process of taking photographs and the documentary ideal, in other words using technology to overcome spatial and temporal barriers."[53]

Bernd and Hilla Becher's four-decade photographic inventorisation of industrial buildings is one of the most important achievements in international architectural photography, and their influence is still apparent; thanks in no small part to Bernd Becher's many years as a professor at the Kunstakademie in Düsseldorf.

1 Eder, J.M.: Geschichte der Fotografie, Halle/Saale: 1923.

2 Benjamin, Walter: Kleine Geschichte der Photographie, in: Das Kunstwerk im Zeitalter seiner technischen Reproduzierbarkeit, Frankfurt/Main: 1966.

3 Frizot, Michel: Neue Geschichte der Fotografie, Cologne: 1998.

4 Ullmann, Gerhard: Einhundertfünfzig Jahre danach, in: Deutsche Bauzeitung 12/1989.

5 Tröster, Christian: Architektur+Fotografie, in: Häuser 2/2002.

6 Busch, Bernd: Friedliche Eroberungszüge – die fotografische Mobilisierung des Orients, in: Daidalos 66/1997.

7 Sachsse, Rolf: Architekturfotografie des 19. Jahrhunderts. Stationen der Fotografie, issue 6, Berlin 1988.

8 Frith, Francis: Die Kunst der Fotografie, in: Kemp, Wolfgang: Theorie der Fotografie, volume 1 (1839–1912), Munich: 1980.

9 Mand, Katja: Das offene Bild. Auf der Suche nach dem "mehr" für die Architekturfotografie, Kassel: 2001.

10 Perego, Elvire: Die Stadt-Maschine, in: Frizot, Michel: Neue Geschichte der Fotografie, Cologne: 1998.

11 Tillmanns, Urs: Kreatives Großformat, volume 2, Architekturfotografie, Gilching: 1993.

12 Nadar, Félix Tournachon: Quand j'étais photographe, Paris: 1900.

13 Perego, Elvire: Die Stadt-Maschine, in: Frizot, Michel: Neue Geschichte der Fotografie, Cologne: 1998.

14 Loydreau, Edouard: De la photographie appliquée à l'étude de l'archéologie, Beaune: 1857.

15 Perego, Elvire: Die Stadt-Maschine, in: Frizot, Michel: Neue Geschichte der Fotografie, Cologne: 1998.

16 Bunnell, Peter C.: Für eine moderne Fotografie, in: Frizot, Michel: Neue Geschichte der Fotografie, Cologne: 1998.

17 Pfingsten, Claus: Zur Geschichte der Dokumentarfotografie, in: Breuer, Gerda: Außenhaut+Innenraum, Frankfurt/Main: 1997.

18 Eastman, George: The Kodak Primer, in: Coe, B.: Das erste Jahrhundert der Photographie, Munich: 1979.

19 Hammond, Anne: Naturalismus und Symbolismus, in: Frizot, Michel: Neue Geschichte der Fotografie, Cologne: 1998.

20 Ibid.

21 Disdéri, André: Die Photographie als bildende Kunst, Düsseldorf: 1864.

22 Ranke, Winfried: Heinrich Zille. Photographien Berlin 1890–1910, Munich: 1985.

23 Mand, Katja: Das offene Bild. Auf der Suche nach dem "mehr" für die Architekturfotografie, Kassel: 2001.

24 Ranke, Winfried: Heinrich Zille. Photographien Berlin 1890–1910, Munich: 1985.

25 Benjamin, Walter: Kleine Geschichte der Photographie, in: Das Kunstwerk im Zeitalter seiner technischen Reproduzierbarkeit, Frankfurt/Main: 1966.

26 Ullmann, Gerhard: Einhundertfünfzig Jahre danach, in: Deutsche Bauzeitung 12/1989.

27 Grefe, Uta: Die Geschichte der Architekturphotographie des 19. Jahrhunderts. Architekturphotographie – Architekturmalerei. Cologne: 1980.

28 Benjamin, Walter: Kleine Geschichte der Photographie, in: Das Kunstwerk im Zeitalter seiner technischen Reproduzierbarkeit, Frankfurt/Main: 1966.

29 Frizot, Michel: Neue Geschichte der Fotografie, Cologne: 1998.

30 The Architectural Record, issue 4/1902.

31 Bunnell, Peter C.: Für eine moderne Fotografie, in: Frizot, Michel: Neue Geschichte der Fotografie, Cologne: 1998.

32 Schmalriede, Manfred: Das Neue Sehen und die Bauhausfotografie, in: Wick, Rainer K. (ed.): Das Neue Sehen. Von der Fotografie am Bauhaus zur Subjektiven Fotografie, Munich: 1991.

33 John Pultz: Strenge und Klarheit, in: Frizot, Michel: 1998.

34 Ibid.

35 Pfingsten, Claus: Zur Geschichte der Dokumentarfotografie, in: Breuer, Gerda: Außenhaut+Innenraum, Frankfurt/Main: 1997.

36 Schmalriede, Manfred: Das Neue Sehen und die Bauhausfotografie, in: Wick, Rainer K. (ed.): Das Neue Sehen. Von der Fotografie am Bauhaus zur Subjektiven Fotografie, Munich: 1991.

37 Frizot, Michel: Eine andere Fotografie, in: Frizot, Michel: Neue Geschichte der Fotografie, Cologne: 1998.

38 Tillmanns, Urs: Kreatives Großformat, volume 2: Architekturfotografie, Gilching: 1993.

39 Pultz, John: Strenge und Klarheit, in: Frizot, Michel: Neue Geschichte der Fotografie, Cologne: 1998.

40 Blossfeldt, Karl: Das fotografische Werk, Munich: 1981.

41 Schmalriede, Manfred: Das Neue Sehen und die Bauhausfotografie, in: Wick, Rainer K. (ed.): Das Neue Sehen. Von der Fotografie am Bauhaus zur Subjektiven Fotografie, Munich: 1991.

42 Frizot, Michel; Haus, Andreas: Stilfiguren, in: Frizot, Michel: Neue Geschichte der Fotografie, Cologne: 1998.

43 Ibid.

44 Sachsse, Rolf: Photographie als Medium der Architekturinterpretation. Studien zur Geschichte der deutschen Architekturphotographie im 20. Jahrhundert, Munich: 1984.

45 Tausk, Petr: Die Geschichte der Fotografie im 20. Jahrhundert, Cologne: 1986.

46 Mand, Katja: Das offene Bild. Auf der Suche nach dem "mehr" für die Architekturfotografie, Kassel: 2001.

47 Sachsse, Rolf: Photographie als Medium der Architekturinterpretation. Studien zur Geschichte der deutschen Architekturphotographie im 20. Jahrhundert, Munich: 1984.

48 Pfingsten, Claus: Zur Geschichte der Dokumentarfotografie, in: Breuer, Gerda: Außenhaut+Innenraum, Frankfurt/Main: 1997.

49 Sachsse, Rolf: Photographie als Medium der Architekturinterpretation. Studien zur Geschichte der deutschen Architekturphotographie, Munich: 1984.

50 Ibid.

51 Sachsse, Rolf: Bild und Bau. Zur Nutzung technischer Medien beim Entwerfen von Architektur, Wiesbaden: 1997.

52 Rice, Shelley: Jenseits des Realen, in: Frizot, Michel: Neue Geschichte der Fotografie, Cologne: 1998.

53 Sachsse, Rolf: Photographie als Medium der Architekturinterpretation. Studien zur Geschichte der deutschen Architekturphotographie im 20. Jahrhundert, Munich: 1984.

Chapter 2
Optical Principles

Axel Hausberg / Anton Simons

54 Lenses and focal lengths
55 Image circles
55 Stitching
57 360-degree panoramas
57 Shifting, swinging and tilting
57 Framing and perspective
60 Adjusting perspective
60 Correcting horizontal lines
63 Contrast
64 High dynamic range imaging
68 Resolution and Sharpness
68 Depth of field
71 Increasing depth of field using the Scheimpflug principle

→ Focal length is one of the most important benchmarks of lenses and lens systems.

The difference between perceiving and seeing is particularly important in architectural photography. Because the retina is curved, we see straight lines as bent, but we know from previous experience that they are straight so we perceive them accordingly. Because architectural photographs with converging lines contradict our subjective experience, they need to be corrected. This is particularly important in the case of churches and other historic buildings.

If you stand in front of a tall building and look up, the main parallel lines of the façade, such as window frames, appear on your retina as converging and bent, but you see them as straight without any conscious effort. If you photograph the structure from the same perspective, it will appear to tilt backwards because your brain does not automatically correct photographs in the same way as it does real life. As an architectural photographer, you should position the camera so that parallel lines on the building appear parallel in the picture.

Apart from using optical means to remove distortion, it is now possible to do this with a computer, as described in chapter 6. A third possibility is to remove it during the enlargement process using the Scheimpflug principle (see section 2.13), but this is rarely done now that photographs can be digitally manipulated.

(2.1) — LENSES AND FOCAL LENGTHS

Camera lenses contain varying numbers of elements and a complex focusing mechanism. Zoom lenses, which are adjustable both for distance and focal length, incorporate several high-precision elements.

If you hold a magnifying glass at a certain distance from a piece of paper and focus the sun's rays on it, the paper will catch light. This is the focal length of the magnifying glass. When you take a photograph, the focal length of the lens plays an important part in the result. It determines the angle of view, in other words where objects must be positioned in relation to the optical axis if they are to be included in the picture. A lens with a wide-angle of view makes objects look smaller – the most extreme case being a fisheye lens – while a narrow angle makes the lens act like a telescope.

To summarise,

→ A short focal length gives a wide-angle of view and a smaller image.
→ A long focal length gives a narrow angle of view and a bigger image.

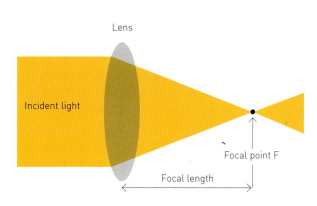

Lenses with a narrow angle of view are called telephoto lenses, and those with a wide-angle of view are known as wide-angle lenses. Those with extremely short or long focal lengths are called super wide-angle or super telephoto lenses. The angle of view is measured between opposite corners of the image. If the focal length is the same as the diagonals of the image, the lens is described as having a standard focal length – not, as is often wrongly assumed, the same angle of view as the eye.

With a small-format camera, a 65-millimetre lens is a lightweight telephoto, whereas with a 4 × 5-inch large-format camera, it is an extreme wide-angle. The angle depends on the focal length and the picture format, and can be adjusted in one of two ways:

1. By changing the focal length using different lenses, converters, or a zoom lens.

2. By selecting the picture format, either by framing or cropping.

If you increase the image format and focal length by the same factor, the image angle remains unchanged. The size of the subject on the film depends on the focal length of the lens. A telephoto lens, which has a long focal length, forms a larger image than a wide-angle lens at the same distance from the subject. The size of the subject projected onto the image plane is proportional to the focal length of the lens at the same distance, so if you double the focal length, the size of the subject on the film or sensor will also double.

Lens	Recommended image scale	Recommended working aperture	Image angle	Image circle diameter	Movement range vertical/horizontal (landscape format)					
					24/36 mm	37/37 mm	33/44 mm	37/49 mm	36/56 mm	40/54 mm
23 mm f/5,6	1:∞	5,6 – 8	112°	70 mm	18/15	11/11	11/9	7/5	3/2	2/2
28 mm f/4,5	1:∞	5,6 – 8	101°	70 mm	18/15	11/11	11/9	7/5	3/2	2/2
35 mm/f4	1:∞	5,6	90°	70 mm	18/15	11/11	11/9	7/5	3/2	2/2
60 mm f/4	1:∞	5,6	60°	70 mm	18/15	11/11	11/9	7/5	3/2	2/2
100 mm f/4	1:∞	5,6	39°	70 mm	18/15	11/11	11/9	7/5	3/2	2/2
180 mm f/5,6	1:∞	5,6 – 8	25°	80 mm	24/20	17/17	17/14	13/11	11/8	9/8

→ This table relates to the Rodenstock HR Digaron-S lens series, designed for digital view cameras. It shows focal length, image circle, image angle and maximum movement range for different image formats.

Regardless of whether you use a small-, medium- or large-format camera, if the focal length remains the same, the subject will always appear the same size on the image plane. The image plane of a large-format camera is so big that a church would fill the whole picture, whereas a small-format camera of the same focal length would only capture a detail of the building, such as the main entrance.

(2.2) —— **IMAGE CIRCLES**

The image circle of a lens is the area which it can include without vignetting – a reduction in brightness or saturation around the edges – or other aberrations. The image circle must therefore be at least as large as the film or sensor format. Specialist tilt-and-shift and other lenses need particularly large image circles to carry out the movements required for architectural photography. Because optical lenses are round, they form circular images, whereas photographs are normally rectangular, so they need to be the right size for the desired picture format to fit inside the image circle.

In a perfect lens, the four corners of the rectangle may be on the edge of the image circle, but this is not the case with tilt-and-shift and other specialist lenses. If the camera is to have sufficient movement, the image circle must be considerably bigger than the image format. If you use a small-format lens designed for a 24 × 36-millimetre sensor format and a 6 × 9-centimetre medium-format housing, the image circle of the lens will be visible on the sensor surface.

→ This lens has a much smaller image angle than the 13 × 18-centimetre film format.

→ The relationship between image format and image circle diameter

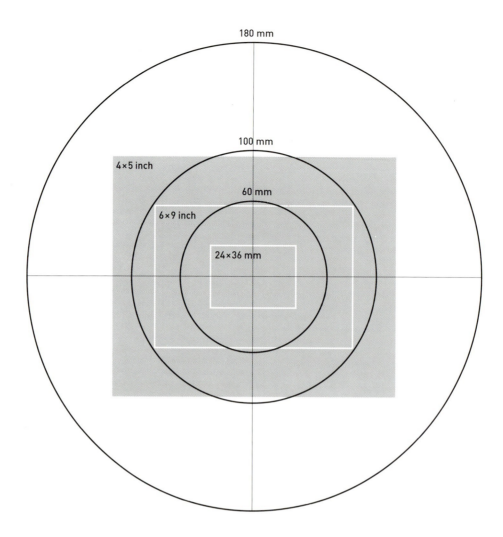

→ The Linhof Technikardan-S camera with the lens raised ...

→ ... and tilted using the Scheimpflug principle

(2.3) — STITCHING

Stitching means taking multiple photographs within the image circle of a lens, and then digitally sewing them together into a single picture. Seamlessly stitching professional-quality pictures in a traditional laboratory was a very elaborate process, which has been revolutionised by digital editing.

The position of the lens remains unchanged while taking the individual pictures, while the camera back and image plane are moved for each one. Stitching is possible only if the camera is mounted on a tripod, and is not suitable for moving objects. There are two good reasons for stitching pictures:

1. It allows you to use the whole image angle of a lens with a small image format, thus covering a larger angle. For example, you can create wide-angle pictures with a telephoto lens.

2. Depending on the number of individual pictures, both analogue and digital stitching give a much larger image area and resolution. Using a digital back with a 39-megapixel sensor and quadruple stitching, it is possible to create more than 140 megapixels of raw data. This gives extremely high resolution of the kind required for posters and building-size advertising hoardings.

In close-ups, and pictures with close foregrounds, you should move the camera's back but keep the lens position unchanged, or you may experience parallax error because the optical axes of the viewfinder and lens are out of line. Move the rear standard horizontally and vertically to increase the image area, or alternatively use a sliding screen, which makes multiple exposures easier. Then combine the parts of the picture to form a whole.

(2.4) — 360-DEGREE PANORAMAS

While panoramas are the bread and butter of landscape photographers, they are unusual in architectural photography. However, they are increasingly being used online for interactive tours of houses, offices, hotels and museums, and can be taken using panoramic cameras.

If you photograph only the occasional panorama, you can do this by stitching pictures together. Make sure the camera is mounted horizontally on the tripod and that the axis of rotation runs through the centre of the front lens element. However, the edges of the individual images should always overlap slightly.

(2.5) — SHIFTING, SWINGING AND TILTING

The image plane can be shifted, swung and tilted in relation to the lens plane.

→ Shifting means moving the lens plane horizontally and/or vertically in relation to the image plane. The perspective is corrected by shifting the lens parallel to the image plane, which also prevents convergence when photographing tall buildings. The image circle of the lens must be sufficiently large to shift, and very large movements are sometimes required. Extreme shifting is possible only with view cameras, and shift lenses offer only limited movement in small-format cameras.

→ Tilting means tipping the lens plane diagonally upwards or downwards in relation to the image plane so that the two are no longer in parallel. This affects the depth of field, for example using the Scheimpflug principle (see section 2.13).

→ Swinging the lens means swivelling its plane in relation to the image plane but, unlike tilting, doing so horizontally to the left or right. This, too, can be used to adjust the depth of field.

→ This stitched panoramic view (Rheinauhafen, Cologne) was made using horizontal shifts to the left and right (figs. 1 and 2). The images were then stitched in Adobe Photoshop (fig. 3) and finally processed and cropped (fig. 4).

Fig. 1

Fig. 2

Fig. 3

Fig. 4

→ Because of parallax errors, the different parts of this stitched photograph do not fit together exactly.

(2.6) — FRAMING AND PERSPECTIVE

Perspective (from the Latin *perspicere*, meaning to look through) is something which is significant for painters and photographers in equal measure. It is a collective term for all the different ways of depicting three-dimensional objects on a two-dimensional surface such as canvas or photographic paper while maintaining the illusion of depth. In photography, perspective depends on the position of the camera and the angle at which the image plane is tilted. Regardless of the focal length you use to photograph an object, if you stand in the same position and shoot at the same angle, the perspective will remain unchanged. So perspective is dependent not on focal length but on camera position; you can change it by moving, but not by switching lenses.

However, focal length does determine framing. This means that:

1. <u>A telephoto lens with a long focal length gives a small image angle and thus shows a small section of the subject.</u>

2. <u>A standard lens with a medium focal length gives a medium image angle and a medium-sized image.</u>

3. <u>The short focal length of a wide-angle lens gives a large image angle and a large image.</u>

Because architectural photography is primarily about depicting buildings as realistically as possible, one of the main challenges it poses is dealing with converging lines and perspective distortion. This is a particular problem in architecture, for two reasons:

→ Most buildings are dominated by horizontal and vertical lines.

→ Buildings are often so large that the camera has to be tilted to fit them in.

If a camera is inclined horizontally or vertically, the subject and sensor or film plane are no longer parallel, so parallel lines in the subject converge towards a vanishing point inside or outside the picture.

If the portrayal is to be as realistic as possible, it is also important to ensure that the ratio of the distance to the height of the subject is as close as possible to that of the viewer's distance from the picture and the size of the object depicted. To deal with this second requirement, before deciding how far away to stand from the subject, you need to think about how the picture will be printed and the purpose for which it is being taken.

Standard focal lengths with image angles of between 45° and 55° convey a natural impression because they are closest to what we see in real life. Telephoto lenses compress space and make objects look nearer. This effect is sometimes used deliberately, for example when selling a house to give the impression that it is close to a forest, or to make a rented holiday home look nearer to the beach than it really is.

Wide-angle shots taken from close to the subject emphasise the foreground and create sharply converging lines. The outlines of buildings become distorted and look excessively large in relation to the centre of the picture, so wide-angle lenses should be used in architectural photography only if a standard lens is not wide enough. Short focal lengths are mainly used to exclude walls, streets or other obstacles which are visible with a normal focal length.

However, architectural photography does use wide-angle lenses, particularly for interiors where it would otherwise be impossible to show a whole room in one picture. Like telephoto lenses, they can also be used to deceive, making small spaces look big, for example in advertisements for homes or recreational vehicles.

The right choice of camera position and perspective can significantly affect the impact of the picture. Buildings are often photographed frontally, with the image plane and façade in parallel, and are normally shown from eye level, which is how we would view the building if we were standing in front of it ourselves. However, there may be good reasons for departing from these basic rules.

→ Move the camera sideways or upwards to block out cars, hedges, fences, neighbouring buildings and other unwanted objects.

→ Use a low camera position to emphasise the height, size and importance of the building. This perspective also allows you to isolate the building from its surroundings and make it stand out.

→ Higher camera positions are particularly suited to views of entire buildings.

→ A telephoto lens compresses the foreground and background.

→ Wide-angle lenses can make small rooms look bigger.

→ The same scene taken with high shift (fig. 1), with the camera tilted upwards so that the parallel lines converge (fig.2) and with the camera in standard alignment (fig. 3).

Fig. 1

Fig. 2

Fig. 3

→ Montabaur station: Converging lines can sometimes create a strong sense of movement.

→ Avoiding converging lines, fig. 1: Use a telephoto lens from a distance.

→ Avoiding converging lines, fig. 2: Raise the camera.

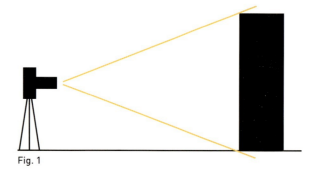

Fig. 1

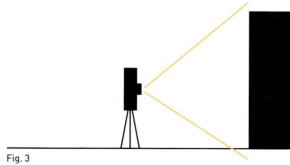

Fig. 3

→ Avoiding converging lines, fig. 3: Use portrait format.

→ Avoiding converging lines, fig. 4: Shift.

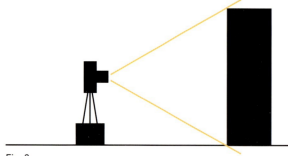

Fig. 2

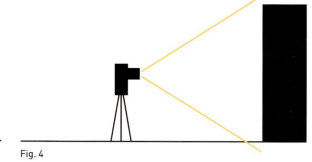

Fig. 4

(2.7) —— ADJUSTING PERSPECTIVE

The vast majority of buildings are vertical, so the architectural photographer has to decide whether to show the verticals in parallel or in perspective. If you look at the building on the ground glass plate of a view camera, you will find the following:

1. If you tilt the camera upwards so that the whole building is visible on the plate, the verticals will taper towards the top. These are known as converging lines.

2. If you hold the camera parallel to the front of the building, the verticals will appear parallel just as they do in real life. However, depending on the height of the building, how far away you are and the focal length you use, the top of the building may be cut off.

3. To stop this from happening, shift the lens upwards.

Photographs with sharply converging lines often have a powerful impact, particularly if you take them from a low angle to emphasise the height of the building.

However, there are no half measures here: the lines must very obviously come together.

If your camera has no movements, there are three ways of preventing convergence:

1. Take the photograph from sufficiently far away to include the entire building with the camera in the parallel position. This can normally be achieved only with a telephoto lens.

2. Choose a camera position high enough to include the entire subject building with the camera in parallel alignment.

3. Use a short focal length and hold the camera parallel and in portrait format. Crop out any unwanted foreground during editing.

If you have a camera with a shift lens, or an adjustable view camera, you can also shift the viewpoint.

Picture editing programs also allow you to edit perspective digitally (see section 6.3).

→ Parallel railway lines converge at a wide-angle when photographed from near the ground.

→ The higher the camera, the smaller the angle.

65 CHAPTER 2: OPTICAL PRINCIPLES

→ This photo shows a frontal perspective with no vanishing points.

(2.8) — CORRECTING HORIZONTAL LINES

If you photograph parallel lines pointing away from you, they will appear to converge towards a vanishing point. This effect is often used in architectural photography to create a sense of depth and three-dimensionality which varies with the choice of camera position and focal length. The shorter the focal length and the closer the camera to the lines, the closer the vanishing point. Conversely, the longer the focal length and the greater the distance between the camera and the lines, the more distant the vanishing point. The lines might include the terrain itself, roads, railway lines and the edges of buildings.

The closer the camera to the beginning of the lines, the wider the angle that they form and thus the stronger the effect. For example, parallel railway lines form a wide-angle when photographed from close to the ground, but not if shot from a bridge. Depending on the subject and framing, the vanishing point may be inside or outside the picture.

Most buildings consist of parallel lines, not just in one dimension, height, but also in width and depth. You can therefore choose the camera perspective to create one, two or three vanishing points, or none. If you include reflections, it is possible to have even more.

If you need to cut out unwanted objects or reflections, you may not be able to take the picture frontally, in which case you will need to shoot it from the side, which again creates a vanishing-point perspective. A view camera allows you to take pictures at right angles with no vanishing points by indirectly shifting the standards into parallel.

1. If you cannot take a picture from the front, take it from as close as possible to a frontal position.

2. Move the rear standard parallel to the front of the building as the principal plane of the subject, so that the building is shown at right angles on the ground glass screen.

3. Place the front standard parallel to the subject. Read the tilt angle from the bearer of the rear standard if possible, though not all cameras allow you to do this.

4. As with any other lens movement, the image circle will shift. Correct this by shifting the front or rear standard sideways.

→ Here, the lines of the building meet at a central vanishing point.

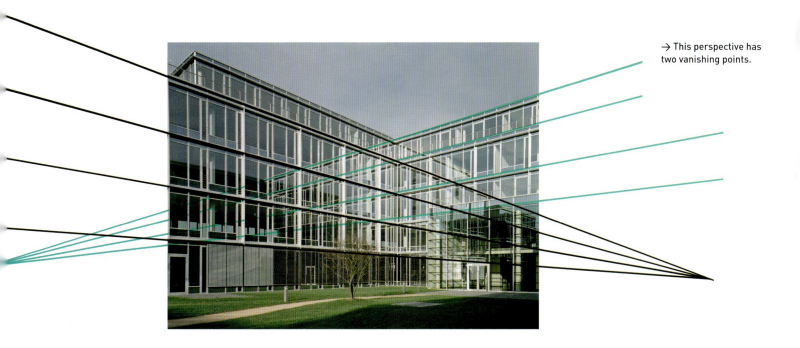

→ This perspective has two vanishing points.

67 CHAPTER 2: **OPTICAL PRINCIPLES**

→ This shot, taken from a very low angle, has three vanishing points.

→ This picture has been exposed so that the darkest parts of the picture are fully reproduced, which means that the lightest areas cannot be.

(2.9) —— CONTRAST

The contrast (from Latin *contra*, against and *stare*, to stand) or dynamics of a picture is the difference in brightness between the brightest and darkest areas. A picture with maximum contrast will have completely black and completely white areas, while pictures with low contrast often consist entirely of grey tones, with no intense blacks or whites. Architectural photographs usually need to reproduce both the brightest areas, such as sky or white walls, and the darkest, often consisting of shadows. In many cases, this is a problem.

The human eye can usually discern contrast easily, because it perceives intensities in logarithmic rather than linear fashion, but photography often struggles to record what the eye sees. In analogue photography these limitations are imposed by the film, while in digital they are caused by the analogue-digital converter, which turns light reaching the optical sensor into electronic signals which can be stored and processed.

Slide films can handle a greater contrast than negative film, and today's digital cameras are even better because they use a non-linear approach to enhancing contrast, in a similar way to the human eye. Low-contrast subjects are easier to photograph than those with high contrast, because they do not force you to decide which information you can manage without by choosing between dark and light areas, and you can always increase the contrast in the laboratory or on the computer.

In the case of extremely high-contrast subjects, however, you still have to choose between reproducing the lightest or darkest parts of the image and set the exposure accordingly – but you cannot have both. If you photograph subjects with more contrast than the film or digital sensor can handle, some of the data will be irretrievably lost, so that it cannot be recreated by editing.

As an architectural photographer, you should always try to take pictures with no more contrast than the film or sensor can manage. In practice this is not always possible, and it is better to underexpose slightly, because dark areas can be enhanced by editing whereas overexposed areas cannot.

→ The exposure chosen for this picture means that even the brightest part of the image is accurately reproduced.

(2.10) — HIGH DYNAMIC RANGE IMAGING

Dealing with high-contrast subjects is a challenge when taking pictures of architecture, just as in other areas of photography. However, it has become easier in recent years with the advent of high dynamic range (HDR) imaging, which is better at handling such situations. Even in natural light, there may be differences in contrast of 10,000 to 1 between the darkest and lightest areas, and if the subject includes a visible light source such as the sun or a lamp, this ratio can significantly increase.

The human eye can detect these wide dynamic ranges, but camera sensors have a range of only around 100 to 1.

HDR simulates human perception, which operates by looking at different areas in a fraction of a second, rather than seeing everything simultaneously. The iris reacts to the brightness of each area, and the brain combines the individual images in the same way as we fuse photographs, to create a single visual impression. As a result, we see both light and shade almost simultaneously. HDR imaging works in much the same way.

These must include at least one image exposed for the brightest areas, and another for the darkest. In practice, photographers create a series of exposures and fuse them into a single picture using HDR software in the camera or on the PC. So the human eye is closer to HDR than to traditional photography, in which the whole subject is recorded on the film or sensor in the same moment. HDR software usually requires at least three different exposures, and the more there are the more finely exposed the result, with four to seven being ideal.

You should leave the aperture and focus unchanged throughout the process, and use the shutter speed to control the exposure. If you use the aperture, the software will have to combine images with different depths of field into a single picture, which creates problems. Likewise, do not move the camera between exposures – as with all architectural photographs, always use a stable tripod – and do not include any moving elements such as people, animals, vehicles, rain, snow and clouds. This means that HDR photography is suitable only for architecture, landscapes, interiors and nature photography, but not for reportage, sport, animals, portraits or fashion.

An HDR exposure should have maximum contrast, colour and brightness. You cannot print out the image file or view it on a traditional monitor; the only way to do this is to reduce the contrast and brightness ranges to create a low- or medium-dynamic-range image. This technique, known as tone mapping and included in most HDR software, creates RAW files which take account of what your eyes can perceive and your printer or monitor can handle, and reproduces both the light and dark areas.

HDR puts an end to bleached-out and underexposed areas, regardless of how extreme the lighting situation, but it is not the first choice for all problematic light situations because the pictures often look hyperreal and artificial. In digital photography, it is usually a better idea to exploit the advantages of the RAW format (see section 4.4).

There are at least three situations where HDR is useful in architectural photography:

1. <u>Church interiors, which need to be photographed so that both the interior and windows are properly exposed. This is a near-impossible task under normal circumstances, because if the interior is shown optimally, the windows become shapeless white spaces. Likewise, if you adjust the exposure for the windows, the rest of the interior ends up being dark.</u>

2. <u>Twilight and night shots outdoors, where until recently it has been largely impossible to reproduce exterior lighting and brightly lit areas as well as shadows.</u>

3. <u>Outdoor shots in bright sunlight. HDR photography can also be useful if you need to photograph highly reflective metal and glass building surfaces which are much brighter than the rest of the picture.</u>

Creating HDR photographs from exposure series, particularly long ones, can require considerable processing power. The most popular HDR programs include the paid-for FDRTools Advanced and Photomatix Pro, the freeware Picturenaut, Photosphere and FDRTools Basic, and the free software Qtpfsgui. Photoshop also has an HDR function, though this is not very good at present in the latest CS5.5 version.

As well as creating single photographs from exposure series, HDR software can adjust brightness and colour.

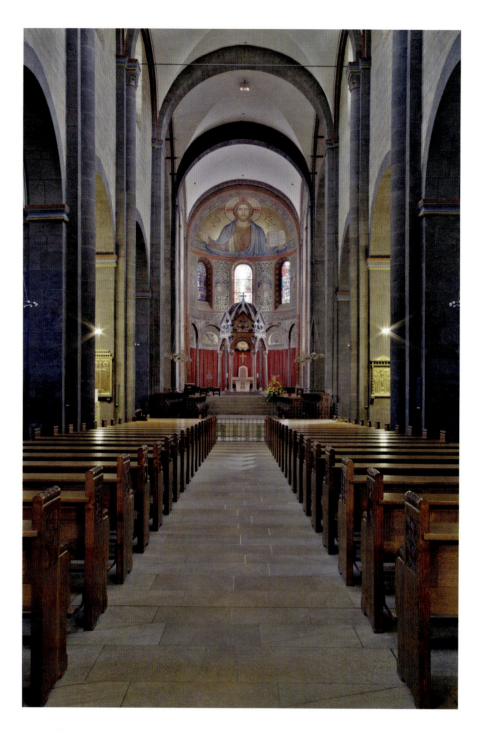

→ This HDR picture was taken from the three individual shots that follow. The seated person has been edited out of the final version.

 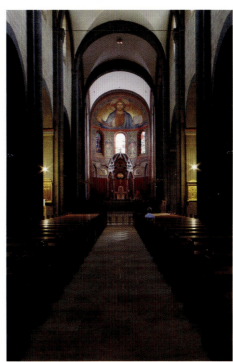 

→ Another HDR photograph created using the three images that follow.

75 CHAPTER 2: **OPTICAL PRINCIPLES**

→ Again, this HDR image of a building by Frank O. Gehry in Düsseldorf is a composite of three differently exposed pictures.

→ The overcast sky reduces the contrast and makes the image less sharp.

← Here, the problem has been resolved by increasing the contrast.

(2.11) — RESOLUTION AND SHARPNESS

Sharpness is not an objective property: it is a subjective impression on the part of the person looking at it. What looks to us like a smooth surface might appear positively cratered to an insect whose eyes have much higher resolution, and whether we see an image as sharp depends on three things:

1. <u>The image itself, and its edge definition in particular.</u>

2. <u>Our eyesight, and especially its resolution: the human eye can resolve a maximum of six pairs of black and white lines per millimetre.</u>

3. <u>Our position, and our distance from the picture.</u>

An image which looks sharp from a particular distance will look blurred if you look at it from closer to, or if you enlarge it and view it from the same distance. It will also look sharper if there are strong contrasts between the textures of the subject:

1. <u>Brightly lit fine details, such as stucco and carvings on pillars, appear in high contrast in direct sunshine or other bright lighting, and sharper than if they had been photographed in diffused light, which reduces the contrast.</u>

2. <u>The boundaries between large high-contrast surfaces look particularly sharp, for example if a whitewashed bay window surround is sunlit and the wall behind it is in shadow. This impression of sharpness remains even if the surface texture of the wall, such as the plaster, is not visible.</u>

Resolution is an important benchmark of lenses, film, digital sensors, and printers. It is defined as the smallest possible distance between two points or lines which they are able to distinguish.

High-quality prints on professional paper normally have a resolution of 150 to 200 lines per inch. Anything above this is perceived by the eye as an even surface, though the eye is very good at distinguishing between different levels of contrast at this resolution.

(2.12) — DEPTH OF FIELD

If the lens and image planes of a camera are parallel, the area between two planes parallel to them will appear in focus, and points behind and in front of this area will be out of focus. The area, known as depth of field, depends on the focal length, aperture and image size, and the distance between the object and the lens.

→ The greater the focal length, the smaller the depth of field.

→ The smaller the aperture, the greater the depth of field.

→ The greater the image size, the smaller the depth of field.

→ The more distant the subject, the greater the depth of field.

Closing down the aperture increases the depth of field, and opening it up reduces the depth of field. The further the image plane from the lens, the larger the area which is in focus. Macro photography often works with depths of field of just a few millimetres, portrait and fashion photography uses a few centimetres, and the depth of field in landscapes may be several kilometres, or even infinity.

The plane within the area of depth of field on which the lens is focused before taking the photograph is known as the focusing plane. At scales of 1:1 and above, the areas of focus in front of and behind this plane are about the same. At smaller scales, the sharp area in front of the focusing plane is always shorter than that behind it.

A rule of thumb in architectural photography, which usually works at medium distance, is that a third of the depth of focus should be in front of the focusing plane, and two thirds behind it.

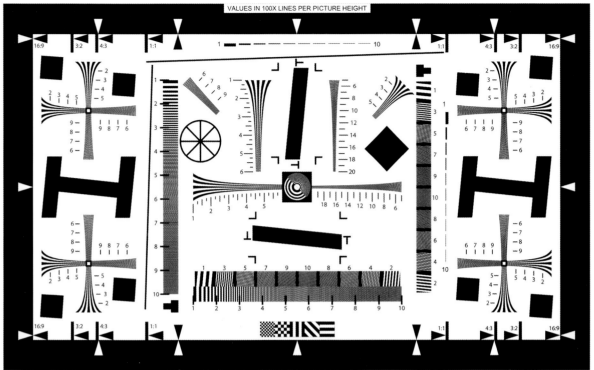

→ This test chart is used to determine the resolutions of lenses, film and sensors.

(2.13) —— INCREASING DEPTH OF FIELD USING THE SCHEIMPFLUG PRINCIPLE

A view camera which is unadjusted or parallel adjusted always shows a plane in focus if it is vertical to the optical axis and thus parallel to the lens and image planes. So, for example, if you are using an unadjusted camera to photograph the front of a building, you will want its entire width and height to be in focus. Problems start to occur if you want to shoot from an angle but keep the entire width of the building to be in focus: if your camera does not allow you to move the image and lens planes, your options are very limited. You can stop down as much as possible to achieve a large depth of field, but this still may not be enough to show the whole front of the building in focus. If you also want to make it stand out by blurring its surroundings, you will need a view camera that allows you to tilt the image and lens planes so that the whole façade is in the focusing plane.

This phenomenon was first described in 1907 by the Austrian army officer and cartographer Theodor Scheimpflug (1865–1911). The rule named after him states that if the image, lens and subject planes are parallel, or intersect at a single point, the whole of the subject plane will be in focus.

Tilting the lens plane allows you to show the whole subject plane in focus, provided it is not parallel to both standards.

Tilting the front or rear standard also tilts the focusing plane, so you can increase the camera's depth of field without stopping down the aperture. This method gives a large depth of field even if the aperture is fully open, so the aperture can be used to make an object in the focusing plane, such as the front of a building, stand out from its surroundings.

Using the Scheimpflug rule makes sense if the subject has a clearly defined principal plane. It applies not only to tilting the image and lens planes, but also to swinging them. Few projects in architectural photography involve swinging, though it is more common in product and model photography.

→ If the front and rear standards are parallel, the focusing plane is parallel to them.

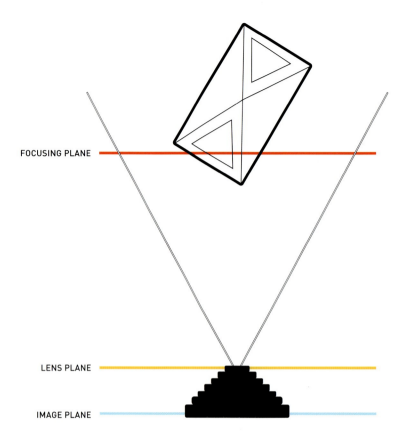

→ Tilting the lens plane allows you to get the whole subject plane in focus even if it is not parallel to both standards.

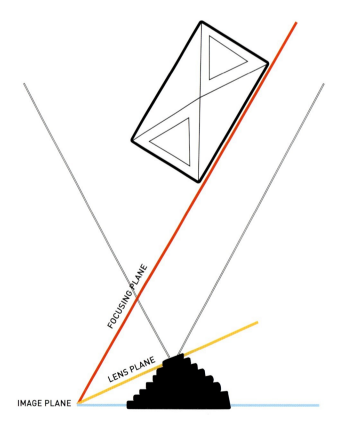

The Scheimpflug effect involves either tilting or swinging the image or lens planes. This creates a variety of effects, each with its own advantages and disadvantages. Moving the rear standard has four benefits:

1. Unlike moving the front standard, it requires only minor focus correction.
2. It allows you to emphasise the foreground by distorting perspective.
3. Since the lens does not move when you adjust the rear standard, the exposure remains unchanged and optimal.
4. It improves the focus, because lenses are designed to achieve optimum focus when they are parallel to the subject.

However, moving the rear standard also has disadvantages:

1. It causes distortion.
2. It makes viewing and assessing the image on the ground glass plate more difficult, because the reflected light rays from the subject meet the plate diagonally rather than in parallel.

Moving the front standard has two advantages:

1. Unlike moving the rear standard, the image on the image plane remains undistorted, so the subject appears natural.
2. The image of the subject on the plate is easier to view and assess because the light rays reflected by the subject are still parallel when they meet the plate.

However, it also has its drawbacks:

1. Unlike moving the rear standard, it requires re-focusing afterwards.
2. It means that you are using not the centre of the lens, but the edge of the image circle. This can cause a loss of brightness and sharpness, though it can be offset by shifting.

Dual and anti-Scheimpflug

In architectural photography, it is sometimes necessary to show a subject plane in focus when it is diagonal and at an angle to the camera. Modern view cameras do this using dual focus adjustment, moving first the horizontal and then the vertical axis. Because the second tilt slightly distorts the first, it requires re-correction. In practice, you can do this in two stages: first tilt the horizontal and vertical axes, and then re-correct each one. Some cameras have a mechanism which makes re-correction after dual focus adjustment unnecessary.

The Scheimpflug rule also allows you to make selective use of blurring. The so-called anti-Scheimpflug principle allows the blurring of unimportant or distracting parts of the image so that only a very small part of it is in focus. This involves tilting the front and/or rear standard so that the limits of focus do not fall within the subject plane, but without tilting the standards in the same direction for so long that their extensions meet at a point, but in opposite directions. To do this, as with using the Scheimpflug effect, you need a lens with a large image circle. The result is clearly visible on the ground glass plate with the aperture open, but you should avoid stopping down to increase the depth of field, so that the blurred areas also appear in the photograph. Dealing with focused and unfocused areas requires practice and experience.

→ This photograph of a subject receding into the background horizontally and vertically was taken at f16 without realigning the camera. Because the depth of focus is so small, only the front row of bricks is in focus.

→ Here the front standard was tilted forwards, which also tilted the focal plane so that all three rows of bricks are in focus.

→ In this photograph, which was taken without realigning the camera, the subject recedes into the background both horizontally and vertically. The shallow depth of field means that only the bricks at the front are in focus.

→ This time, the front standard was tilted forwards, which also tilted the focal plane so that all the bricks, from the bottom foreground to the top background, are in focus, with the exception of those on the left and right.

→ Here, the front standard was also swung, shifting the focal plane to the main plane of the subject, which inclines towards the right background.

→ Here, the camera is not realigned, but the depth of field is sufficient for the whole subject to be in focus.

→ Using anti-Scheimpflug with the rear standard emphasises the red sign on the left and the roundabout, but moving the rear standard distorts the proportions.

→ Setting the rear standard using anti-Scheimpflug also emphasises the sign and roundabout, but maintains the natural proportions.

→ Careful use of anti-Scheimpflug can achieve some striking effects.

Chapter 3
Equipment

Axel Hausberg/Anton Simons

92 Photographic disciplines
93 Architectural photography with a small-format camera
95 The view camera
97 Digital backs
103 Lenses for analogue and digital architectural photography
109 The tripod
110 The tripod head

It is the photographer who creates the photo, not the camera. An effective image first takes shape in the mind of the photographer. Nevertheless, equipment plays an important role in photography alongside ability. Photographers need equipment which will allow them to realise their ideas. All equipment presents certain opportunities, but also has its limitations; all equipment has its strengths but also its weaknesses. The aphorism that a chain is only as strong as its weakest link also applies to architectural photography. To take a perfect photo, the equipment must be right – the camera, the lens, and the data or film back, the data format, the image processing system and the print facility. It is not absolutely necessary to work with the most expensive equipment to achieve top-class results. The requirements are that you have mastered your craft and are aware of and make use of the options offered by your equipment. However, you must also know its limits.

(3.1) — PHOTOGRAPHIC DISCIPLINES

The range of separate disciplines gathered under the heading of photography is surprisingly wide. This affects not only camera housing, lenses and other items of equipment, but also the preferences and strengths of the photographer.

Animal photography
It is without a doubt true that of all photographers, those who photograph animals need the most patience. They also need to be physically fit, so that they can carry heavy equipment over long distances without getting out of breath. It also helps to have some DIY skills, as anyone taking photographs of wild animals should be able to build a shelter or a hide. Animal photographers should enjoy quiet and solitude, but on the other hand need not be gregarious or chatty. An animal photographer's equipment consists primarily of a small-format camera and high-speed lenses with extremely long focal lengths.

Fashion and people photography
Someone who photographs people should be sociable, communicative and able to deal sensitively with their fellow human beings. Their equipment consists of a small and/or medium-format camera and high-speed, medium telephoto lenses. Reflecting telephoto and wide-angle lenses are also used occasionally. Fashion photographers also need a portable flash unit and folding diffusers and bouncers.

Portrait photography
In order to take portraits which show people in natural and unforced attitudes, the photographer must be able to build confidence and a close relationship within a short time. Not a lot of equipment is required: a small or medium-format camera with a small telephoto lens and a studio flash unit are sufficient.

Press photography and photojournalism
Press photographers and photojournalists must be fast, mobile and flexible. They should be able to grasp a situation quickly and – particularly important – have an instinct for the right moment. Furthermore, they should not be shy and retiring, because it is rarely possible to take good photos from the second row. A small-format camera with lenses in the wide-angle to short telephoto range and an integrated flash unit are the press photographer's tools.

Sports photography
Successful sports photographers should enjoy sport and be familiar with the basic rules of the sport they are photographing. Another useful skill in sports photography is the ability to press the shutter button at the right moment. The equipment consists of a small-format camera, telephoto lenses, dedicated flash and a monopod. Taking photographs in sports halls demands very high speed lenses.

Food and product photography
Of all the photographic disciplines, food and product photography makes the most demands on the photographer's ability to compose an image and to handle both natural and, primarily, artificial light. Unlike photojournalism and sports photography, product photography consists largely of preparation. Anyone who wants fast results will never feel at home in this discipline. The technical equipment includes a medium-format or, better still, a view camera with movements and a studio with a flash unit. Food photographers need a whole arsenal of accessories, including black card to cast a shadow over individual parts of the composition and mirrors to brighten and create highlights.

Car photography
Cars are nothing other than large products. Planning, preparation and lighting play as big a part in the photography of cars as they do in food and product photography. Much time is spent subsequently processing the images on the computer. Anyone who chooses this discipline must be enthusiastic about technology. The equipment required to photograph cars as the customer expects them to appear is very similar to the product photographer's equipment. The flash units required are considerably larger.

Landscape photography
A landscape photographer should be friendly, love nature and culture and, like an animal photographer, be impervious to the weather and enjoy travelling. Fitness and an adventurous nature are also desirable. The landscape photographers' equipment consists

of a small-format camera with lenses ranging from wide-angle to telephoto and a tripod. However, there are also landscape photographers who work with medium and large-format equipment.

Architectural photography

What are the desirable characteristics in photographers of architecture and what sort of equipment do they need? They should have a passion for architecture and an eye for the infinite variety of light effects. While a sports or press photographer has to have an instinct for the right moment, an architecture photographer must have a eye for perspective and light.

(3.2) — ARCHITECTURAL PHOTOGRAPHY WITH A SMALL-FORMAT CAMERA

Amateurs who would like to go into architectural photography should on no account invest large sums in a view camera straightaway, although anyone planning to earn their living with architectural photographs will not be able to avoid buying a view camera with movements sooner or later. This is because the specification for architectural photos is to show the building as realistically as possible – particularly with regard to avoiding deformation or distortion.

This means that straight walls should look straight and rectangular door frames should not appear bowed. The photographer will soon be brought up short by the limits of a non-adjustable small-format camera without any special lenses when asked to meet these specifications. Good architecture photos can result as long as it is not necessary to tilt the camera up or down. That is to say, if the optical axis is perpendicular to the image plane and parallel to the surface of the earth. If you have a good lens, with a fixed focal length if at all possible, you can reproduce very good views, such as the skyline of a city, with a small-format camera. Many small-format lenses however, particularly cheaper products and zoom lenses, can cause barrel or pincushion distortion. This is not noticeable as long as the photographs are of organic forms – people, animals, plants or landscapes – but as soon as straight lines are a major feature, these distortions spoil the effect of the image. It is also possible to use a small-format camera to take very good photographs of material surfaces or architectural detail – door fittings, handles, and fixing of façade elements, for example.

A small-format camera is also excellent for images which are not intended to be true to life, but which offer an artistic representation of architecture. However, these are the limits of what can be achieved in architectural photography with a small-format camera without special lenses.

Small-format camera with shift lenses

The shift function allows the lens system to be moved relative to the plane of the film or sensor within certain parameters. The tilt function allows the lens system to be tilted relative to the plane of the film. This makes techniques available to small-format cameras which originally were the preserve of view cameras. Nikon brought out the first shift lens for small-format cameras in 1961. Nowadays there are also combined shift and tilt lenses. If you decide to buy a lens of this type, then choose a combined lens with a rotating mount because they can be adjusted in any direction.

First-class images can be created with a small-format camera and a shift lens. Furthermore, it is possible to carry out a large range of assignments. What are shift lenses for? In most cases, they are used to avoid perspectival distortion or to take photos with the perspective of a frontal image when the camera is offset to the side. Shift lenses are also suited to preventing the photographer and the camera from appearing on the photo of a reflecting façade.

The lens manufacturer Schneider in Bad Kreuznach, for example, offers shift lenses for cameras from Canon, Nikon and other well-known manufacturers. Lenses with 24 or 28 millimetres focal length are recommended. A new lens of this kind currently costs between 1,000 and 2,500 euros. Lenses with tilt and shift mechanisms make higher demands on the quality of the optics than do normal lenses. The most important condition for allowing the lens system to be shifted and tilted relative to the image plane is that the special lens has a larger image circle than a traditional lens. This is the only way to avoid shadowing and light fall-off at the edges of the image.

Lenses always make the image sharpest in the middle; it becomes less sharp towards the edges. A lens with a large image circle requires particularly sharp edge definition. This makes tilt and shift lenses larger, heavier, more complicated and much more expensive than traditional lenses; in some cases they are more expensive than lenses for view cameras. Nevertheless, these optics can never offer the resolution, sharpness and adjustment options of a view camera. If you seriously intend to practice architectural photography in the long term, it might be more economical not to buy a special lens for a small-format camera and instead to invest in a view camera. There are relatively affordable used shift cameras available with a fixed lens, such as the Plaubel Proshift and the Cambo Wide. Neither of these cameras is still manufactured today, but they almost achieve the performance of a view camera. Silvestri still manufactures both 6 × 9 centimetres and 5 × 5 inches cameras. Their earlier models are also available at very low prices in

→ It is perfectly possible to take photos like this with a small-format camera.

→ The PC-Super-Angulon 2.8/28 millimetres from Schneider is a typical shift lens for small-format cameras.

the second-hand market. However, the better alternative is the purchase of a used view camera.

(3.3) — THE VIEW CAMERA

For professional architecture photographers who want to be equipped to deal with every situation and assignment, there is no way of avoiding purchase of the view or large-format camera. This holds true equally for analogue and digital photography. The more widely spread digital technology becomes, however, the more the range of equipment and consumables for analogue photography shrinks. Only Kodak and Fuji remain from the numerous colour film manufacturers who were in business up to a few years ago. They produce colour film in the following flat-film formats:

→ 9 × 12 centimetres
→ 13 × 18 centimetres
→ 4 × 5 inches
→ 8 × 10 inches

There is still a number of manufacturers of black-and-white film. In addition to the two mentioned above, these are Ilford, Foma, Adox, Rollei, Maco, Forte and Bergger. The range of formats in black and white flat film is larger than that of colour film. Common formats are:

→ 9 × 12 centimetres
→ 13 × 18 centimetres
→ 18 × 24 centimetres
→ 4 × 5 inches
→ 5 × 7 inches
→ 8 × 10 inches
→ 11 × 14 inches
→ 10 × 12 inches
→ 20 × 24 inches

This prompts the question of which of these many formats one should choose. A photographer with professional ambitions should choose one of the four colour formats. It is possible to create black-and-white images from coloured material using digital technology, but the reverse is impossible. Apart from that, the demand for black and white photos has fallen so much in the past few years that they now only seem to have a part to play in artistic architecture photography. The larger the film material selected, the less manageable and more voluminous and heavy the equipment. Megaformat equipment is currently offered at bargain prices on the second-hand market.

However, one should not be tempted by it. As the size increases, so do the costs of film, development and digitalisation. Furthermore, many professional laboratories are no longer able to process very large-formats. Photographers are then forced to develop film themselves. Film formats of 13 × 18 centimetres and above are used almost exclusively by photographic artists, enthusiasts and collectors. It is possible that the 4 × 5 inches format will survive in the long term; it is the most practical and most widely used.

The range of lenses for this format is also the largest on offer. Another argument against the mega formats is that it is quite impossible to use their resolution potential. A 4 × 5 inch slide is sufficient to produce enlargements in the City Light (118.5 × 175 centimetres) and Mega Light (356 × 252 centimetres) formats.

Since the lens manufacturers Schneider / Kreuznach and Linos / Rodenstock produce wide-angle lenses with a focal length of 35–47 millimetres with large image circles and good capacity for adjustment, more compact 6 × 9 centimetres cameras, such as the Technikardan 6 × 9 and the Arca-Swiss F-Line metric 6 × 9 are good alternatives.

There are also compact systems in large- and medium-format from Alpa, Silvestri, Gilde and Cambo etc. These systems, which are available as rangefinder or focusing cameras, allow limited shift options. If you work with one of these cameras, you must accept that they offer fewer movement options. It is not only because of their large image formats that view cameras are the first choice for architecture photography; tilt effect and perspective manipulation are more important.

View cameras are fundamentally of a modular construction. The individual components, such as the front and the rear standard, can be replaced as required and moved independently of each other. This makes these systems versatile, upgradeable and future-proof. Depending on the task in hand, it is possible to combine different lenses and other accessories. These include adapters which slide to allow you to switch between viewing the ground glass and readiness to capture the image. This obviates the need to disassemble the film or digital back and prevents these modules from being dropped and sustaining damage.

For example, it is possible to install a medium-format back to a view camera to save material costs or, similarly, to replace the back of a 8 × 10 inch camera with a 4 × 5 inch rear standard. Another reason why modular systems are future-proof is their option of replacing a film back with a digital back. Nowadays, manufacturers offer adapters for almost every conceivable combination.

→ Normally, perspective distortion is to be avoided. Occasionally, however, it makes for an impressive photo.

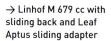
→ Linhof M 679 cc with sliding back and Leaf Aptus sliding adapter

Structure of a traditional view camera

Traditional view cameras, such as the Linhof Kardan, are constructed as follows. They have a rear standard with a ground glass on which to look at the image, a front standard, which holds the interchangeable lens, and a flexible, lightproof bellows which connects the two standards. Within these U or L-shaped standards it is possible to move the brackets holding the lens and ground glass or digital back horizontally and vertically. The ground glass is the projection surface made of translucent material which in single lens reflex and view cameras is used to check the image composition and detail and to focus the lens.

The standards are mounted on a rail or a tube. They can thus be moved forwards and backwards on this optical bench to calibrate the distance between them to the focal length of the lens and to adjust the focus. The rear standard is always used for fine-tuning the focus. The standards are not fixed directly to the optical bench but are attached by hinges. These hinges enable the photographer to position the standards perpendicularly or to tilt them horizontally or vertically. This allows the perspective to be manipulated (see section 2.7 Adjusting perspective) and the focus to be pulled (see section 2.11 Resolution and sharpness).

The longer the focal length of the lens, the greater the distance required between the standards. The distance between the standards for a lens with a focal length of 1,000 millimetres is one metre. However, such long focal lengths are rarely used in architectural photography. They are required to photograph a building from a long way away, for example. Long extensions present the photographer with a number of problems:

→ A second tripod is required to keep the optical bench stable; the two tripods are mounted at the front and at the back behind under the optical bench. However, a second tripod means extra weight to transport.

→ Furthermore, several bellows are required. Auxiliary standards are necessary to connect them with each other and to prevent them sagging.

→ The longer the extension, the more light is lost between the front and the rear standard. A wider aperture and/or a longer shutter speed is required to compensate. This loses sharpness and also increases the likelihood of camera shake and motion blur.

Many photographers make no distinction between lenses with a long focal length and telephoto lenses. For small-format photography, this distinction is indeed of no importance. With a view camera, on the other hand, that is not the case. Lenses are normally constructed so that their focal length is equivalent to the distance between the standards. However, with telephoto lenses, the extension is much shorter than the focal length due to the design of the lens. Telephoto lenses have been developed with the aim of reducing the problems of long focal lengths with compact construction. Neither a second tripod nor additional bellows and standards are required to take photographs with a view camera and a telephoto lens. A disadvantage of telephoto lenses is their high price compared to traditional designs. Their image circle is also somewhat smaller. That is not significant, however, because telephotography does not require a lot of movement options.

When taking wide-angle photographs, it is necessary to reduce the distance between the standards so much that the options for movement are limited. The retrofocus lens was developed to solve this problem. This permits longer distances between the film and the lens planes despite shorter focal lengths.

(3.4) —— DIGITAL BACKS

The development of digital backs for view cameras is lagging behind that for small-format cameras. Possibly the most important reason for this is that the market for view cameras is much smaller than that for non-specialist cameras. However, there are now sophisticated digital solutions on offer for architectural

→ Tilt movements in a front standard (Linhof Kardan GT)

→ Swing movements in a front standard (Linhof Kardan GT)

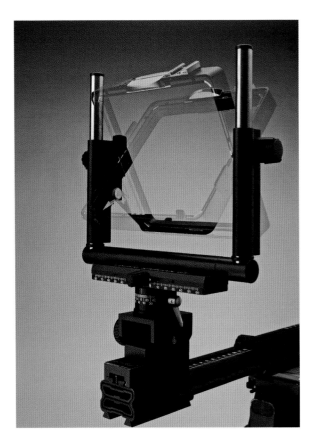
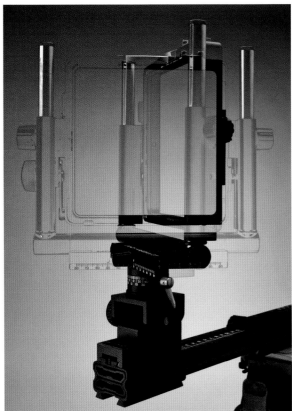

photography. This includes view cameras which were designed for use with digital backs and digital backs adapted for view cameras which were originally made for use with flat or roll films. The size of the sensors in these digital backs now ranges from 40.4 × 53.9 millimetres and resolutions are up to 60 megapixels.

Because digital backs have a much smaller sensor format, lenses with much shorter focal lengths are required to photograph the same angle of view as when film backs are used. Manufacturers have now developed special lenses for digital photography. These include wide-angle lenses with image circles with shift options which make them suitable for architectural photography. However, for technical reasons, these still offer fewer movement options than those of analogue lenses with the equivalent focal lengths. This is because the lens manufacturers are not keeping up with sensor development. The first lenses developed specially for use in view cameras with digital backs were intended for a sensor size of 24 × 36 millimetres. In the meantime, digital backs with sensors of 40.4 × 53.9 millimetres have become standard. First generation digital lenses cannot be used with these new backs.

When digital backs are used, all the camera components must be finished with particular precision, because in a small-image format distortions have a greater impact than in large-formats. For example, if a 90-millimetre wide-angle lens is tilted on a 4 × 5 inch analogue camera by 10 to 15 degrees, this is equivalent on a 35 millimetre digital lens on a view camera with a sensor size of 40.4 × 53.9 millimetres to a tilt of only 2 to 5 degrees. This shows how precisely the mechanism in a camera with a digital back works and how accurate the setting options must be. Furthermore, the construction of digital cameras must be extremely robust so that they do not lose precision during transportation and rigorous day-to-day use.

The maximum exposure duration on most digital backs is limited to 60 seconds, because longer exposure times would create much more image noise with the Dalsa sensors that are frequently used. There are also digital backs which allow exposure times of up to one hour. This is useful to know if you want to use long exposures.

Compared to analogue systems, however, digital backs also offer benefits and open up new opportunities. Digital equipment is much more compact and is lighter than analogue equipment and it permits the photographer to work faster and more fluidly. It is not necessary to take instant photos because the images can be inspected straightaway in the display. When

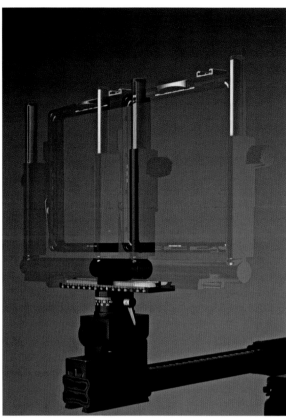

→ Rise or vertical shift in a front standard (Linhof Kardan GT)

→ Lateral or horizontal shift in a front standard (Linhof Kardan GT)

large quantities of photographs are taken, furthermore, the running costs are lower, because there is no need for instant film, development, digitalisation or retouching. In digital photography, the results are available much more quickly than with analogue systems. This applies particularly to HDR photos.

Like many small-format digital cameras, digital backs are now able to display real-time histograms. In digital photography, histograms are the visualisation of statistical frequencies of grey and coloured values, the dynamic range and the brightness of a potential subject or image. The X-axis of a grey value histogram shows from left to right the brightness levels of the image from black to white. It is possible to read off from the Y-axis how many pixels of the photo are shown in the grey value in question. The further to the left the curve peaks, the darker the image and vice versa.

Real-time histograms allow the photographer to detect under- and overexposure before the photograph is taken and to correct the settings. Due to the intrusive ambient light and because the displays on the camera backs are relatively small, histograms created at the site of the image can only provide guidance, however. Histograms produced during post-processing under standardised conditions on a large computer monitor can be analysed much more precisely (see Chapter 6 Post-processing).

Moving from film to digital backs requires the photographer to become accustomed to different shutter settings. This is because depth of focus is lost when the aperture remains constant with the size of the subject on the image plane. That means that when a subject is photographed on a small-format camera with aperture f8, the depth of focus is greater than if you photograph the same subject with the same aperture on a large-format camera. To achieve the same depth of focus it is therefore necessary to close the aperture more when using a view camera.

With 4×5 inch film format, ideal definition is achieved with f16 or f22. Depending on the quality and the model of the lens, unsharpness due to diffraction is only detectable from f32. Because the depth of focus increases as the image format becomes smaller, the ideal focal range with a digital back with a 36×48 millimetre sensor is at f8. For photographs taken at twilight or for time exposures, this has the advantage that the exposure time can be reduced. Unsharpness due to diffraction is noticeable at f16 in this format.

The sensitivity of the sensor should not be set to higher than 200 ISO/ASA when photographing with digital

→ Linhof Kardan GT with extremely long extension on two tripods and with an auxiliary standard.

→ Linhof Techno with telephoto lens and telephoto extension

→ Linhof Techno with wide-angle lens and wide-angle bellows

→ Analogue
Schneider Super
Angulon 5.6/90 XL

→ Rodenstock
HR Digaron S
5.6/23 millimetres

backs, otherwise there is a risk of digital image noise spoiling the photograph. This is caused by incorrect electrical information which is transmitted from the analogue-digital converter integrated in the digital back. Images with digital noise look like prints of high-sensitivity, grainy film. It is particularly obvious in shadowy and dark sections of the image, especially when it has been greatly enlarged.

Live View und Live Preview

Almost without exception, digital small-format cameras offer the option of live view or live preview. These are optical systems which make it possible to monitor the image detail and sharpness on a display.

The electronic image signal is transferred in real-time from the sensor to the display. This is of particular interest for architectural photography as live view systems can superimpose lines for aligning the camera over the image shown in the display.

Digital backs for view cameras with live view without a PC connection, however, are not yet available. The reason for this is that CMOS (complementary metal oxide semiconductor) sensors are fitted in digital small-format cameras, while sensors with CCD (charge-coupled device) technology are fitted in digital backs for view cameras.

One of the many advantages of CCD sensors is that they achieve better definition than CMOS sensors. Their major weakness is that they do not permit live view. Therefore, a photographer using a view camera and a digital back is forced to make the image settings on a ground glass which is the same size as the sensor in the back, that is, 40.4 × 53.9 millimetres max. Anyone used to working with a 4 × 5 inch ground glass will find that this is a considerable step backwards. Furthermore, adjusting a camera with a digital back is much more difficult than a camera with a 4 × 5 inch film.

The development of live view displays with a minimum size of 4 × 5 inches and the option to superimpose a grid would represent real progress for digital architectural photography.

(3.5) —— LENSES FOR ANALOGUE AND DIGITAL ARCHITECTURAL PHOTOGRAPHY

In every respect, good architectural photos are only achieved with high-end components, because these photos, irrespective of the training and experience of the photographer, are the product of the camera with all its components, from the scanner to the print facility. However, even the best and the most expensive back, for example, only delivers mediocre results if the quality of the other camera components is not up to scratch. This applies particularly to lenses, which must meet the demands of the back used.

The most important principle of architectural photography is that the geometry of architectural subjects is reproduced accurately. This means that doors, windows etc. like the outlines of right-angled buildings, should be shown with no distortion.

→ Phase One P 65+ digital back

→ The sensor for the digital back P 65+ from Phase One

→ This photo exhibits digital noise, because the ISO value of 3,000 set on the camera was excessively high.

Anyone working as a professional photographer of architecture, therefore, requires lenses that function free of distortion. A distortion is a fault in the lens which causes straight lines to appear bent. Barrel distortion is the name given to a lens fault where the lines curve outwards; pincushion distortion is where the lines curve inwards.

In landscape photography, where organic forms dominate, such distortion is not seen as a problem; it is unacceptable in architectural photography. So that they meet these stringent requirements, lenses for architectural photography must be developed, calculated and manufactured with great care. Furthermore, lenses intended for architectural photography must have particularly large image circles, as shift and tilt are not otherwise possible.

For digital photography, it is usually not sufficient to equip a camera with a digital back and then continue to work with traditional lenses. This is because digital lenses differ in a whole series of details from analogue lenses.

Analogue and digital lenses
The light-sensitive particles in the film emulsion used in analogue photography are equivalent to the cells in the sensor in a digital back. Unlike the irregularly arranged film particles, the sensor cells are ordered in a grid. The film emulsion consists of crystals which are arranged irregularly and in several layers one on top of the other; sensor cells, on the other hand, are rectangular, usually square. The even arrangement of the sensor cells is the cause of a number of image faults which can all, however, be avoided: colour cast, centrefold, colour fringe, moiré effect and aliasing.

→ Colour cast
Colour cast is an image fault with particular significance for architectural photography. This fault manifests itself in colour changes in some areas which can occur when shift and tilt movements are used with digital backs. These colour changes usually become magenta or green towards the edge. Colour cast varies from lens to lens but, like a fingerprint, remains the same for each individual lens. The manufacturers of digital backs supply software with them which can compute this fault out of the image file for each individual lens.

→ Centrefold
Centrefold is an image fault which occurred very frequently in digital photography until a few years ago, but is no longer significant. It had the effect of making one half of the image appear lighter than the other. It was due to the design of the sensor.

→ Colour fringe
Colour fringe is another fault that can occur when a digital back is used; it manifests itself as a thin coloured line along sharp edges with a high level of contrast. It is caused by the lens. Wide-angle lenses with retrofocus which are calibrated for analogue photography are particularly prone to this fault. It does not occur in lenses calibrated for digital photography.

→ Moiré effect
The moiré effect is an image fault that manifests itself in lines which occur when several patterns with evenly arranged lines, squares or grids are combined. This effect can arise, for example, when a façade faced with a metal grille is photographed with a digital camera. The higher the resolution of the sensor, the lower the tendency to moiré. A slightly softer image lowers the risk of moiré as does stopping down, but on the other hand this increases the unsharpness due to diffraction. The photographer must therefore weigh up the advantages and disadvantages.

There are several ways to prevent this fault:

→ With a filter positioned in front of the sensor, which makes the image softer and less sharp.

→ Using a digital back with a microlens array

→ Subsequent removal with an image processing program.

In photographic technology, a microlens array refers to the placing of a microscopically small collecting lens in front of each sensor cell. These lenses straighten light coming in at an angle and increase the light yield. Digital backs with microlens arrays are used to create perfect images of fine textures, such as the surfaces of textiles and furs, in people and fashion photography. Microlenses ensure that incoming light that would hit the area between the sensor cells is bundled and directed to the sensor cells.

→ Aliasing
When an image is captured, that is, when an analogue signal is digitalised, the rectangular shape of the sensor cells and their grid arrangement can cause diagonal lines in the subject to appear like steps. This imaging fault, which is called aliasing or the stair step effect, creates patterns which are not present in the subject. Photographers try to combat aliasing in the same way as for the moiré effect – with softer lenses or with anti-aliasing filters which are fitted immediately in front of the sensor and which ensure that the subject is projected onto the sensor with minimum unsharpness.

→ Barrel and pincushion distortion illustrated on the same subject

→ Structure of a sensor cell

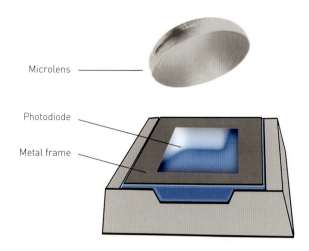

Microlens

Photodiode

Metal frame

Film and sensor thickness
Commercially available digital sensors are around 35 micrometres thick. The light-sensitive layer of a slide film, on the other hand, is around four times thicker. Unlike the film, which is slightly convex in the camera housing and which never lies completely flat on the film pressure plate, the surface of a digital sensor is almost completely level. As a result of these differences, analogue cameras forgive certain tolerances in the lens, whereas digital sensors make much higher demands on the precision of the optics and the mechanics of all the camera components. Because the focus on a digital camera must be adjusted much more accurately than on analogue equipment, digital cameras must be manufactured with considerably greater precision.

Protective glass
Between the back lens of the photographic objective and the light-sensitive layer there is only air in film photography, whereas in digital backs, the light also has to penetrate a 1–2 millimetres thick glass pane which protects the sensor from dust and contact. When the light reflected by the subject enters the protective glass and leaves it again, it is refracted twice more than it is with a film camera. This and reflections on this protective glass can cause colour shifts, ghosting and lack of definition. These effects can be avoided, however, if the lenses for digital photography are calibrated differently from lenses for film photography. Some of the most important parameters which can be varied when the lens is designed are the types of glass and the combination of glass types, the number of lenses and the finish on the lens surfaces.

Colours and sensors
In digital photography, each pixel is composed of different brightness values of the three base colours, red, green and blue. It would therefore be ideal if each sensor cell could image the brightness values of all three colours. For technical reasons, sensor cells can only capture one colour. Therefore, the cells in the image sensors are grouped into fours. A tiny colour filter is placed in front of each of these cells. Usually two cells in each group of four are sensitive to green, one to blue and the fourth to red. In order to nevertheless to have a full RGB value for each pixel, the camera software calculates the missing colour values for each sensor cell from the colour values of its three neighbouring cells. This process is called colour interpolation.

On strongly contrasting edges, this colour interpolation can cause orange- or cyan-coloured seams. However, these can be avoided if the lenses are calibrated specifically for digital photography. There are also software filters that remove the colour seams with calculations. These filters are integrated in the digital back.

Finally there is the option to remove the colour seams in subsequent image processing on the PC. Incidentally, not every individual light-sensitive particle on a film is sensitive to all three base colours, but similarly only to one colour. Films therefore consist of three layers; each layer is sensitive to a different base colour.

Sensor size and focal length
Digital sensors are currently made with a maximum area of 2.2 square millimetres. On the other hand, 4×5 inch flat film has an area of 10 square millimetres. As a result, a wide-angle lens designed for 4×5 inch flat film becomes a slightly telephoto lens when it is combined with a digital sensor. Whether one can take wide-angle, telephoto or normal photographs with a lens is not determined only by the lens but by the lens-image format combination. Although it might be possible to continue to use an analogue lens with a digital back, this principle makes it impossible to take wide-angle digital shots with these analogue lenses in every instance. Therefore, when converting to digital photography it is not possible to avoid the acquisition of wide-angle lenses with extremely short focal lengths. Furthermore, lenses for digital backs must have a higher resolution than lenses for film backs, because the same imaging capability must be delivered by the smaller area. With large-format film a resolution of 40 line pairs per millimetre is sufficient, but digital backs require at least 60 line pairs per millimetre.

Compendium shades and lens hoods
A lens hood, also known as a lens shade, is an important accessory in both analogue and digital photography – just how important is frequently underestimated. Its function is to prevent light falling onto the film

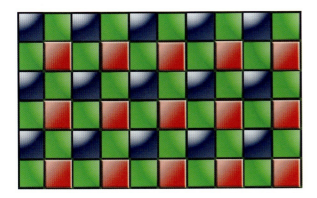

Format	Diagonals (mm)	Focal length (mm)					
24/36 mm	43,3	23	35	47	55	72	90	120
36/48 mm	60	17	25	34	40	52	65	87
40/54 mm	67,4	15	22	30	35	46	58	77
6/7 cm	91,2	11	17	22	26	34	43	57
6/9 cm	100,1	10	15	20	24	31	39	51
4/5 inch	150			13	15	20	25	33
5/7 inch	210						19	25

→ Schematic representation of a Bayer sensor

→ Comparison of focal lengths for various image formats

or the sensor from the side, because it is reflected on the lens or the lens barrel. These reflections result in colour falsification, a reduction in the contrast and lens flares, that are lens-shaped, circular or anular seams of light. All such reflections are extremely detrimental to the quality of the image, frequently making photographs unusable. It is very damaging that the lens flares often cannot be seen on the ground glass or the display. This is particularly the case in bright ambient light, which is why lens hoods are available for many lenses. They are generally rigid tubes of metal or plastic that are attached to the lens with a threaded, bayonet or click-on fixing. The hoods are either supplied with the lens or can be bought as an accessory. There are no lens hoods available for view camera lenses, however. These are protected from flare with compendium shades. A compendium shade is an attachment in the form of an adjustable bellows which can be made longer or shorter depending on the angle of view.

(3.6) —— THE TRIPOD

In small and medium-format photography, tripods are used to make shake-free photos when light conditions are poor – indoors, in twilight or darkness. For architectural photography with a view camera, a tripod and a tripod head are essential.

→ It is only possible to carefully position the camera and subsequently check the image with a tripod.

→ A tripod helps the photographer to wait for the right moment allowing activation of the shutter to be delayed until all the moving elements in the surroundings that are relevant to the image composition provide a harmonious whole. These are primarily humans, animals, vehicles and the light.

The tripod and the tripod head must not only be able to support the camera, but they must also be sufficiently robust to cope with a sudden gust of wind, for example. When in doubt, it is better to err on the side of heavy and large rather than small and light; the larger a tripod, the more stable it is.

Tripods usually have three adjustable legs. When buying a tripod, ensure that the central column can be extended a long way. A tripod should allow photographs to be taken from a ladder at heights of over two metres. An extendable central column might lower the stability slightly, but allows the camera to be positioned higher. There are also models on which the central column can be fitted upside down. This makes it possible to use the camera at very low levels. An alternative are tripods with legs that can be widely angled; they also allow "worm's eye" views.

Traditional tripods show their limitations in exposed camera positions, which can only be reached with a ladder or a cherry picker. For such situations, clamping tripods are available which can be attached to the rung of a ladder.

→ Compendium lens hood for the Linhof M679CS

→ Hasselblad HDC 28 mm with lens hood

Tripods are made of various materials. Aluminium, titanium, carbon and wood are those used most frequently. Each of these materials has strengths and weaknesses, particularly in respect of weight, torsion resistance and vibration absorption and also temperature and weather resistance:

→ Wood damps vibrations particularly well, but is heavy.

→ Titanium and carbon are relatively light, but expensive. Carbon is furthermore not very robust: a bang against a hard edge will cause irreparable damage. If only one leg is damaged, it can be replaced, but at considerable cost.

→ Aluminium is a good compromise in terms of weight, stability and price.

(3.7) —— **THE TRIPOD HEAD**

The tripod head connects the camera with the tripod. Whereas cameras used to be fixed directly to the tripod head with threaded screws, nowadays most photographers use quick-change adapters.

An adapter plate is screwed permanently to the underside of the camera. A click-on system allows the camera and the tripod head to be attached firmly to each other within seconds, with no need for tools. Magnesium, plastic and die-cast aluminium are usually used to make tripod heads. There are four different types of tripod head available commercially today:

→ Ball joint tripod heads
→ Two-way heads
→ Three-way heads
→ Geared heads.

Three-way and geared heads are suitable for architectural photography. Ball heads are not recommended, because all the camera dimensions are fixed with a single screw requiring all the axes to be released when adjustments are made. There is a risk that when one axis is adjusted, the other two will also be adjusted involuntarily, which initially goes unnoticed. Two-way heads only move in two directions. They allow the camera to be tilted sideways and inclined vertically. Portrait-format photographs are not easy to achieve. This type of head is suitable mainly for video recordings.

Three-way heads make the third dimension accessible to the photographer as each individual dimension can be adjusted cleanly one after the other. There is no danger that when one dimension is adjusted, another axis is moved. Geared heads are the most convenient and very accurate, but they are also the most expensive. They have no screws which need to be released for adjusting and then tightened again to fix the head in place, but have self-retaining tooth-wheel drives. They can be adjusted with particular precision

→ FOBA system tripod with clamp

so that the camera can be positioned accurately to within a degree. This is particularly crucial when taking photographs with the relatively small sensor formats in digital backs. Professional tripod heads nowadays all have a water or circular level with which to align the camera and a scale on the rotational axis which makes it easier to take panoramic photos.

→ The aluminium ALFAE tripod from FOBA

→ Video head MA 701HDV from Manfrotto

→ Cube C1 from Arca-Swiss

→ Geared head MA 410 from Manfrotto

→ Ball-jointed head with circular levels from Hensel

Chapter 4
Photographic practice

Axel Hausberg/Anton Simons

119 Realisation
136 Light and Lighting
166 Exposure metering
169 The RAW format

→ This house is of a traditional wooden construction.

→ This house is of an open construction type.

Once a commission is finalised, the next step is to prepare and organise the photograph. This begins with agreeing a time and date with the caretaker, the tenant or the owner of the building. You are unlikely to manage without the help of the building manager or the caretaker, particularly in the case of large properties. For example, you will need to have access to all the rooms to ensure that they are clean, tidy and available and possibly to switch the interior or exterior lighting on or off or to rearrange the blinds. Then you should find out about the route and on-site parking, if necessary make a room booking and hire an assistant and prepare yourself as well you can for the session. In order to schedule the shoot, it is important to find out about the direction the building faces in relation to the sun.

Then, it is time to get your equipment ready. Load films and instant film cartridges, collect together the lighting equipment, pack charged batteries and replacement fuses, flash lamps and memory cards. Add to this: flash tripods, a small ladder, an extension cable and a power strip. It is also important to pack comfortable, practical clothing appropriate for the time of year and the weather.

If you are intending to photograph a building with which you are not familiar, you should find out about the light situation on site before the actual shoot takes place. There are several ways to do this. For example:

1. Travel on the day before you plan to take the photo, or at least before sunrise in order to familiarise yourself with the building and its orientation towards the sun.

2. Early on, ask the architect or the owner or builder to send you a drawing of the building with an arrow indicating north.

3. Use Google Maps or Google Earth to find out about the property's orientation and surroundings.

4. Calculate the position of the sun with the appropriate software.

Once you have arrived on-site, leave your equipment in the boot of your car, so you can walk around unencumbered and familiarise yourself with the building you have come to photograph. Observe it from more than a photographer's point of view; try to answer a few important questions which are immediately associated with the architecture.

→ How is the building positioned in the landscape and in the space available?

→ To what extent are the forms of the building derived from its function and what is the role played by aesthetic considerations?

→ How is the building constructed? For example, skeleton or room module construction? Does the building reveal that costs, deadline or convenience played a part in planning and construction?

→ Which materials and colours dominate the façade (the outer shell of the building)?

→ Is it an open or a more closed construction? Characteristics of open construction are large windows and light interiors into which one can see from the outside.

→ Does the exterior of the building indicate what is inside it or does the building hide its interior behind a decorative façade?

→ Is the building connected to its surroundings? Does it merge into the landscape or the surrounding buildings in terms of its shape, colour and material, for example. Does it contrast with them or does it give the impression of being a separate world?

→ Do the orientation and shape of the structure and the materials used indicate that the owner/builder found the ecological aspects of the construction important?

→ What attitude towards life and what self-image did the architect or the builder/owner want to express?

→ What does the building reveal about the builder/owner?

→ Was the architecture of the building important to the owner/builder or was its appearance secondary or not important at all?

→ Was innovative architecture important to the builder/owner or did he or she consciously choose traditional architectural elements?

→ Does the building make a simple and old-fashioned or a modern impression?

→ Does the building make an inviting impression or does it make you want to walk away? Large uniform façades with small windows are typical of unapproachable buildings.

→ Do the builder/owner and the designer want the building to be perceived as a work of art or as a functional construction?

→ The construction here conveys the impression of preferring to remain apart from other people.

→ With older buildings, it is often worth looking to see if the building, the front garden, the back garden and the immediate surroundings harmonise or whether they have developed separately over the years.

→ Has the building been modernised or extended? How has the architect dealt with the old parts of the building? Are they still recognisable? Has the effect of the original building been destroyed, or has it developed organically?

With the findings and impressions of this exploratory exercise in mind, the task now at hand is to find the best possible views of the building and the best places from which to take photos for the designated purpose. The ambient light, the current weather, any imponderables and building work, either on the building itself or in the neighbourhood, should be taken into account when deciding on specific times and places. It is fundamentally advisable to make every effort to find an unusual position from which to take the photo; this is the most reliable guarantee for a high-quality photo. It is often possible to position the camera on a wall, a garage roof, in the window of a neighbouring house or on a ladder. A fork-lift truck is also an option: this will lift a pallet with the camera, tripod and the photographer up several metres. If there is absolutely no unusual camera position to be found, take the photograph from a normal standpoint and use other means to try to achieve a result with which the customer is satisfied – by composing the image in a particular way, for example. When testing the effects of potential camera positions on the image, it helps to close or cover one eye and hold a rectangular frame in front of the other.

A single image is, however, unlikely to do justice to an architectural work. A representative series of illustrations includes the following views as a minimum:

→ A general picture of the building in its surroundings

→ A view of the front façade with entrance area

→ An angled perspective conveying an idea of the shape and dimensions of the property

→ Modern wooden frame estate houses

→ Some façade details such as attractive items, interesting structures and unusual shadows.

If elements in the vicinity intrude check whether they can be removed, possibly just temporarily. Otherwise, it might be possible to eliminate them by manipulating the perspective or in post-processing. It is best to photograph the interior in the order in which a visitor gets to know the property.

→ The entrance area

→ The hall

→ The stairway

→ The corridors

→ Individual rooms

→ Where appropriate, detailed views of the interior, the reception area, a seating area or a fitted kitchen, for example.

(4.1) —— REALISATION

Having now developed a shoot plan, it is time to use the camera. Unlike a fully automatic small-format camera, a view camera forces the photographer to adopt a disciplined and systematic approach, to be careful and also, to a certain extent, to act slowly. The camera compels him or her to think carefully about the details of the subject and the perspectives, to compose the image for optimum effect and to adjust the standards accurately.

Unlike in an SLR camera, in the view camera the subject is shown upside down on the ground glass. Photographers who find it difficult to get along with this can buy modules with an angled mirror which rotates the image. There are normally grid lines printed on the ground glass of a view camera. Other manufacturers etch lines into it. These grid lines help to align the camera with the vertical and horizontal lines of the building.

There are three other important features available to the photographer to help with observing and controlling the way the subject is imaged on the ground glass.

→ An unusual modern apartment building

→ Planning constraints limited the architect's creativity here.

→ This canteen is anything but functional.

→ This is a converted and extended functional structure from the 1960s.

→ A typical example of a conventional new building

→ Form and materials were given careful consideration in the design of these estate houses.

→ This estate conveys the impression of being a small world on its own.

→ Like the farm on the next two pages, this wooden museum building blends perfectly with its surroundings.

→ This series of images of a detached house starts with a photograph taken from the street outside ...

→ observers are conducted through the entrance hall,

→ ... and the stairway

→ ... into the kitchen and finally

→ ... into the garden, with a view of the back of the building.

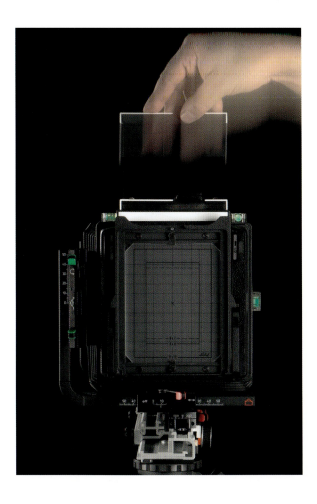

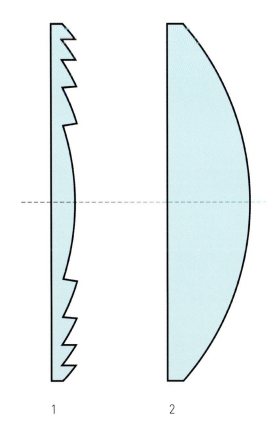

1   2

→ Grid lines are used to align the camera with the vertical and horizontal lines of the building.

→ Fresnel lenses (1) are lighter and take up less space than traditional collecting lenses (2).

The Fresnel lens, or more precisely the Fresnel step lens, is used to brighten the relatively dark ground glass image. This disk-shaped collecting lens takes its name from Augustin Jean Fresnel, who invented it around the year 1822. The structural principle of the Fresnel lens, which was originally used in lighthouses, is to reduce the weight and volume of large lenses.

This is particularly effective with lenses with short focal lengths which are normally very thick and heavy. The Fresnel lenses for view cameras can therefore be clamped directly to the ground glass.

The focus cloth prevents ambient light from hitting the ground glass and making it more difficult or, in the blazing sun of high summer, impossible to assess the image on it. Finally, the magnifier allows the camera to be focussed precisely with adjustment of the standards.

When adjusting the camera, you should always proceed in the same way and check each change to the camera settings on the ground glass before making the next adjustment. If you find that you encounter seemingly insurmountable problems with adjusting the camera, it is frequently helpful to zeroise all the settings and start the following procedure from the beginning:

→ First, set up the tripod and the camera.

→ Place the camera approximately into position.

→ Now, adjust the height.

→ These magnifiers are used for assessing the image on the ground glass and on slide film.

→ If you have not already done so, set all the camera settings to zero.

→ To ensure that the image shows the correct perspective, use a spirit level (usually integrated) to ensure the camera is completely straight.

→ Then, using the grid lines on the ground glass or the lines superimposed on the display, align the camera with the important horizontal and vertical lines of the subject.

→ Then, also using the grid on the ground glass, correct the sideways movement of the camera housing.

→ It might be necessary to return the desired image to the ground glass between the steps by shifting one or other of the standards.

→ Now, use the magnifier to focus. To do this, bring two planes into focus – first the frontmost plane and then the hindmost plane that you want to have in focus. Then divide the difference between these two planes into three and set the focus on the line between the first and second thirds (see section 2.12 Depth of field).

→ To check the depth of focus, stop the lens down to the working aperture. If the depth of focus is not sufficient, check whether it is possible to pull the focus using the Scheimpflug principle (see section 2.13 Increasing depth of field using the Scheimpflug principle).

This is normally the case when one dimension dominates, that is, when a main plane in the subject needs to be in focus. Examples are wide façades which extend diagonally into the depth of the image, from right front to left back or vice versa. With subjects that extend into several dimensions, the Scheimpflug principle only helps when one of them is given priority.

→ If it is not possible to achieve the desired depth of focus with stopping down and application of the Scheimpflug principle, the scale of the image is reduced by increasing the distance of the camera from the subject.

→ If the composition needs to be corrected again subsequently, use the rear standard and not the front standard. Changes to the front standard would impact on the perspective.

→ Then, check the corners of the ground glass to ensure that the image of the subject is free of light fall-off. Another possible, but less widely used method of checking is looking through the lens at the working aperture setting.

→ Now, remove any intrusive elements – rubbish, dustbins, barriers etc from the image.

→ Also check whether all the windows of the building are closed, whether the blinds are open and the rooms evenly lit.

→ Measure the exposure to determine the shutter speed required.

→ It is now time for an analogue instant photo or a digital test shot.

→ Releasing the shutter for the actual photo follows careful examination of this shot and correction of lighting, composition, focus and filters.

A single, well-composed architectural photograph can take from half to a full hour – even longer if artificial lighting is required for an interior shot.

(4.2) —— LIGHT AND LIGHTING

Whilst it is impossible to take a photograph without a camera or a lens, they are nevertheless not the most important elements in photography. Light is much more important; the word "photography" literally means nothing other than "drawing with light". Apart from the perspective, it is primarily light that determines the effect of an image. This includes the brightness, the direction and the colour, the mood and the distribution of light. The most important source of light for a photographer of any kind is the sun; this applies particularly to architectural and landscape photography. That is why, as an architectural photographer, you should familiarise yourself carefully with the effect on the image of the position of the sun, the weather conditions, the time of day and year and the direction in which the building faces.

The sun as a source of light
Sunlight varies greatly, depending on where the photograph is being taken, the time of day and the weather conditions. Over the course of the day and as the seasons pass, its colour temperature changes and, because the angle of the rays varies, so does its character. When there is no or little cloud cover, the sun casts shadows. The sun, which is a light source almost like a spotlight, is infinitely distant in optical terms. It therefore emits a bundle of parallel light rays. Furthermore, because it is so intense, sunlight is very harsh and the difference between light and shade when the sky is clear is frequently so pronounced that no photographic medium can reproduce it easily. Working with slide film is particularly difficult in direct sunlight. Slide film cannot cope with more than four f-stops between light and shade.

You should also measure the dynamic range before every shot when you use negative film or a digital back in extreme light conditions. If it is larger than four f-stops then you must expect that the shade and/or highlights will not be defined. You must then decide whether you can live with this deficiency or whether you can or want to take measures to combat it. There are three options:

1. To brighten the shade with flash

2. To use HDR technology

3. To use the RAW format, which is only available in digital photography and allows management of much wider dynamic ranges than is possible with film.

The best solution, however, is to take the photograph under more balanced light conditions, where the dynamic range does not exceed four f-stops. This is possible:

1. In diffuse light

2. With the sun behind you

3. When the sunlight falls from the side at a time of day or year or under weather conditions when the shadows cast are not too harsh

4. When the sunlight falls from the side and the deep shadows cast by the subject do not appear in the image.

Each of these four options has an impact on the effect of the image. Light falling on the front of the subject reduces the depth of the image, whilst a subject with areas of heavy shade emphasises the impression of plasticity and three-dimensionality.

In accordance with the way humans habitually look at an object, in the western hemisphere the effect of an image is improved when the sun shines on the subject slightly from the left. When the light comes from this angle, the colour value scale is larger than with flat frontal light. In addition, shapes and surface textures on the subject are best modulated under these circumstances.

The influence of the time of day on the effect of the image

The morning is often the most favourable time to take photographs: at this time of day, the number of microparticles in the air which diffuse the light is at its lowest. Furthermore, in the morning – and the evening – the differences in brightness in the light and shaded areas are least pronounced. On the other hand, the shadows at this time of day, particularly when the light falls from the side, are very long. Another factor that is also quite important in photography is that the colour temperature of the light changes over the course of the day: in the morning and the evening, the colours are warmer than at midday.

The influence of the seasons on the effect of the image

In principle, it is possible to take good architectural photos at any time of the year. However, you should take into account that the angle of the sun's rays changes over the course of the year. The sun is highest in the summer, so shadows are at their shortest. In winter, the reverse is the case. When buildings are to be photographed with their surroundings, with the front or back gardens, for example, the season will be reflected in the vegetation. The season is therefore significant when the intention is to take photographs for postcards, brochures or catalogues to be used for tourism purposes. A farm in the Black Forest, for example, looks at its most attractive when the geraniums are trailing long stems from the balconies and photographs of winter sports areas are naturally always taken when snow has just fallen.

The influence of the weather on the effect of the image

Most architectural photos are taken in good weather, when the sun is shining in the summer. However, this can give rise to light situations in which the contrasts border on the unmanageable. In these cases, a cloudy sky and diffuse light can be advantageous. If a shower of rain occurs when you are carrying out a photographic commission, it is often worth waiting for it to pass before you take the photograph. Summer rain cleans the air; when it is over, the colours glow particularly clearly and streets and pavements look as if they have been varnished.

One also has the option of creatively including reflections from puddles in the composition. Furthermore, interesting light moods often precede or follow summer showers.

Pleasing images can be created even when the weather is not perfect. Schedules also sometimes force you to take photographs in bad weather. You should therefore practise making the best of a whole range of light and weather situations. Particularly with rather average and standard buildings, the weather can help to create unusual photos. On a foggy November morning, a house on a residential estate that is not really worth a second glance might well become the subject of photo that would excite some interest. Taking photos at twilight can also set the scene effectively for drab buildings. Apart from

→ The same building in direct ...

→ ... and in diffuse light.

→ Strong contrasts lend depth to this front view.

→ Visibility is best in the morning.

that, twilight and night-time photos provide a way to solve the problem of wet or patchy façades.

Twilight and night time photos
A photograph taken at night is primarily significant for its special impact. When a heavily glazed high-rise building is fully lit up, maybe even in colour, a twilight shot can look very spectacular. Photos taken at twilight can also make a very bold statement. What this means is that you can create very effective images of buildings of little particular architectural merit with the aid of twilight photos. A twilight photo is a possible alternative if it is important to set a building apart from its unattractive or insignificant surroundings. Twilight photos can also be useful for lighting reasons. A twilight photo can be the solution when a customer is determined (possibly also at short notice) to have a photo of the side of a building on which, due to the time of day or the year, the sun does not shine. Similarly, if a building is situated among tall trees.

Twilight photos are also a solution when a customer requires a photo on which no people, animals nor vehicles can be seen. Intrusive objects which move through the image, such as passers-by or vehicles, can be eliminated by the long exposure times that are typical of twilight photos. These range, for a film sensitivity of 100 ASA, f16, from two to eight minutes.

During daylight, it is possible to achieve the same effect by placing a dense grey filter in front of the lens to increase the exposure time. It is also possible to remove intrusive objects in digital post-processing. Determining the exposure for twilight photos is not easy and requires considerable experience. Exposure bracketing is employed by those wishing to play safe.

When the photo is taken, it is important that the building is lit from the inside – through windows, glass doors or a glass façade. It is often advisable to supplement the light in the room with a flash or artificial light. If it is possible to see into the rooms through the windows, then they should be dressed with furniture and plants, and also with people working, playing or sitting. Photos of this nature must be planned in good time and thorough preparations made. It is important for the effect of the image that the silhouette of the building stands out from the night sky. A twilight image is therefore ideally balanced when it does justice to the rooms inside, when the house outlines remain visible and when the sky and the surroundings are washed in a mystical blue.

Sometimes, additional lighting for the façade cannot be avoided. Indeed, "Night time photo" as a description is misleading. Taking photos in complete darkness only makes sense in exceptional cases. In total

→ At dawn or dusk, the brightness values are well balanced.

← The midday sun creates strong contrasts and makes colours glow.

→ In spring, the green colours of nature are particularly rich.

→ Under the summer sun, colours are at their strongest and contrasts most pronounced.

→ Golden October seen from its best side.

→ The cool colours of winter...

→ Shortly after a shower, colours are particularly strong and the streets appear varnished.

→ For this twilight shot, all the interior lights were switched on and additional lamps were placed on the balconies.

→ Light trails can enliven photos taken at twilight.

darkness it is only possible to take photos of buildings which are lit up from outside, such as churches and museums. Because artificial light changes natural colours, attention must be paid to the colour temperature in such colour photographs.

The best twilight photos are taken during dusk or just before dawn. There is a longer window of opportunity at this time during the summer than in the winter. At the dark time of the year, twilight only lasts a few minutes and there is only time for one perfect photo. A lot of experience is required to find the right time for a night photo and a bit of luck is often needed as well. Therefore it is advisable to take a whole series of photos of the building in question, starting in the early evening. The correct time is somewhere between dusk or dawn and darkness.

It need hardly be mentioned that a stable tripod, a timer and a shutter release cable with a toggle should be used for long exposure times. Passing vehicles can be made invisible by dodging with the hand, a piece of card or by interrupting the exposure. Note that vehicles with lights often look very interesting; photographers use them to provide features and enliven a scene.

When deciding whether to buy an analogue or a digital camera, take into account that not all digital camera backs are suitable for long exposures by any means; many only permit exposures of up to 30 or 60 seconds.

The weather also plays a part in twilight photos. It is not possible to take good architectural photos in pouring rain because the drops of water look like unattractive stains. Immediately after a heavy shower, however, the air is usually exceptionally clear and wet streets offer interesting reflections and mirroring. A covering of snow can also be helpful because it brightens up the area and extends the twilight. With new buildings, the snow can also help to hide unfinished outside areas.

Artificial light

When taking architectural photos indoors, you should use the natural and artificial light as far as possible. Generally speaking, when architects design an interior nowadays, they develop lighting concepts that support the effect they want the room to project. Additional artificial light sources would impair this effect.

However, if there is no natural or artificial light or if it is inadequate, there is no alternative but to use continuous or flash lighting. Additional light should be utilised discreetly so that it does not intrude on the natural effect of the room, but instead helps to bring out the best in it.

Unlike product photographers who need to have a large and varied stock of lights and lamps so that they can carry out any assignment required of them, architectural photographers normally only need a relatively small range. However, in no other photographic discipline does one learn better how to use light, and architectural photographers would be well advised to learn from a product photographer. In order to manage in any lighting situation, you should practise handling various flash and artificial lighting systems, light shapers, bouncers and other aids, which are also used in product photography.

Light direction

In photographic training and study, light direction is considered very important and much time is devoted to it. It starts with the trainee or the student painting or photographing wooden jointed puppets, shop window mannequins or even just simple geometric shapes – cones, pyramids and spheres – which have been lit with a single source of light. The light source is then carefully repositioned and the changes to the shadows and light effects are observed and documented in photographs. Various objects are also placed in front of the light source to change the shape of the beam and bundle or scatter the light. Later, several light sources are used and bouncers are also placed in position. Once these initial exercises have been internalised, the budding photographer moves on to using suitable lighting and auxiliary apparatus to deliberately create specific mood lighting – dramatic, flat and three-dimensional, for example.

→ This twilight shot was exposed for more than four minutes.

→ If the photographer had exposed it for any longer, it would not have been possible to see the moving cars.

→ Dramatic lighting is created with a dark underlying mood and sharply contoured light from behind or from the side. Light coming from different directions should also create a stronger impression of depth in the image, so that the observer's gaze is constantly taken from one plane to another. In nature, it is possible to see dramatic light moods during or after thunderstorms when the sunlight is filtered or split by the clouds. Direct sunlight falls – contrary to the otherwise usual visual experience – as it would from a spotlight onto or behind the object. And puddles and wet asphalt and façade surfaces reflect the sunlight and create the impression that there are additional light sources. Anyone determined to photograph a certain building in a storm does of course require a great deal of patience and luck.

→ The impression that a two-dimensional image represents a three-dimensional space is based on an illusion which is created from the interaction of light and shade. A flat image results from using just one light source, which is positioned behind the photographer. Deep shadows should be avoided. If that is not possible, the shadow is brightened with additional light or reflective surfaces. Flat architectural photographs are rarely required, but are sometimes helpful; when detaching an interesting building façade from boring surroundings, for instance.

→ A three-dimensional image is created by staggering light and shade into the image. Using several image planes to create depth strengthens the impression of spaciousness and three-dimensionality.

Another exercise for architectural photographers is to study and photograph the effects of an interior under different lighting conditions at different times of the day and at night. This allows them to support the natural effects of the interior with the careful use of light.

→ Compact flash kit consisting of a generator and three flash units with a softbox, a reflective umbrella and a normal reflector

→ Portable generator set with a flash head and a standard reflector

→ This flash generator from Hensel delivers 3,000 watt-second.

→ Softboxes create a soft and widely spread light.

→ Flash head with a normal reflector as a light shaper

→ Here, the ball is lit from above only. The lower half is brightened by the surface on which it stands.

→ Here the ball is lit only by a light source placed to the left. Nevertheless, it conveys a very three-dimensional impression.

→ In this image, the ball is also lit from the front. A light from top right increases the tension.

→ Diffuse exterior light makes this façade appear flat. It is the interior lights that give this image depth.

→ The dim light makes the fortress-like architecture seem even less inviting.

→ The changes from light to shade lend this image a particularly three-dimensional effect.

→ The background has been brightened with a flash in this image.

→ This subject is illuminated only by the daylight entering the room.

→ Here the existing artificial light has also been switched on.

→ Night mood with existing artificial light and flash in the background

Difficult lighting situations
Architectural photographers frequently encounter these three difficult lighting situations when shooting indoors:

1. <u>All of the subject is too dark.</u>

2. <u>There is a mix of natural light and artificial light in the subject.</u>

3. <u>The subject is lit by artificial light only.</u>

How should the photographer deal with these lighting situations?

<u>Dark subject</u>
The first problem is that the interior to be photographed is too dark overall. Sometimes, it is so dark that even long exposure times are insufficient to deliver a photo with a spatial effect; the existing light only permits dreary, flat images. Sometimes there are some light sources in the rooms, but they are not enough to light the room adequately. Underground stations and railway station concourses at night are typical of such lighting situations, as are churches. Smaller areas can be brightened with a flash or artificial light supplied by the photographer; HDR photography is helpful for larger areas (see section 2.10 High dynamic range imaging) as are images in RAW format (see section 4.4 The RAW format). Additional light can be used so that the image has a more natural appearance. In order to avoid overdoing the light, it should be used very carefully and sparingly. Experience shows that the risk of an unnatural-looking image increases with the number of light sources used. Good results are often achieved with an indirect flash reaching the subject via the ceiling or walls. Furthermore, it is possible to create more depth and highlights with light shapers.

Usually two lamps or flashes are sufficient to light a small residential room. On the other hand, photographing factory floors and other large spaces might well require two dozen lamps or flashes. When using continuous light, you should ensure that it is not too bright and that the colour temperature of the light harmonises with the subject. If necessary, work with a lens filter or with filter films in front of the light sources. Flashlight is generally neutral. Modern flashlight units also have adjustable lights which permit the effect of the flash to be controlled accurately. Sometimes, it is worth trying to do without the flash, and lighting the subject with the adjustable light. It should go without saying that lamps, tripods and other photographic accessories should not be seen in the picture, but nevertheless it happens frequently. Look carefully at magazine photographs of festively laid tables with much tableware, cutlery and polished candelabra and it is not rare to discover reflections of the photographer. Nowadays, errors like these can be corrected easily with digital post-processing, but in analogue times, the images were frequently rendered useless.

If you do not have enough lamps or flashlights with you, or if you are in a particular hurry, one option is to use a mobile light source. This can be a flash, but also a torch or another kind of continuous lighting. In such a case it is important that the colour temperature is neutral or goes well with the subject. However, this method only works if it is so dark that it is possible to work with exposure times of several minutes. With the shutter open, the light is carried around the subject, where possible not in the image view, to illuminate surfaces and details. However, working with a mobile light source is almost impossible without testing the exposure. When carrying out these tests, you should note precisely the direction, the distance and the light strength used to illuminate each surface and detail. This is the only way to repeat a lighting exercise without any changes or with more light. Nevertheless, when using a mobile light source it is never possible to deliver the light effect as accurately as when using a stationary light. Generally speaking, the rules to apply when using a mobile light source are never to direct the light at the camera and never at oneself. Photographers working with mobile light sources frequently should note that many digital backs are unsuitable for use with them because they only permit maximum exposure times of 30 seconds.

→ All the lights in the room have been switched on here and all the side doors opened to allow light in. Furthermore, there is indirect light from a flash to the left at the rear and from the side rooms.

↘ No additional light was used for this unevenly lit shot.

→ The direct flash has "killed" this shot.

→ This shot was brightened with a mobile light in addition to the existing light.

Blended light

The second most frequent difficult lighting situation is blended light. When lights with different colour values come together in one image subject, photographers refer to mixed light. The most frequent case is when daylight mixes with artificial light. Blended light can help to liven up a subject; the challenge is frequently to balance the mix of colour temperatures and to adjust the camera to the colour temperature of the light where the image is being captured. A grey card is required to do this; a sheet of white paper can be used if necessary. The grey card is placed in the area to be photographed in a position which should subsequently be represented in neutral colours in the image. There are two options:

1. The preferred solution is to calibrate the camera, then remove the card before releasing the shutter.

2. Alternatively, the neutral point can be set to the card in post-production. After the colour has been corrected, the image is retouched to remove the card.

The safest way to achieve a photo which conveys a true impression of the colour is to use a colour temperature meter. After the desired colour temperature has been set on this device, it displays the colour value of the filter that must be used to achieve this colour temperature. The basic equipment for a professional should therefore include a filter holder and the five lowest densities filters each in the colours cyan, yellow and magenta.

Thanks to the options offered by digital post-processing, it is nowadays frequently easier to correct the colour in post-production on the computer. Because this allows each individual colour to be weakened or strengthened separately, even better results can be achieved than with the use of photographic filters. Another point in favour of correcting colours on the computer: the high prices of colour temperature meters and lens filters. Even when a colour temperature meter is used, colour correction in post-production is frequently unavoidable.

Artificial light

A third potential lighting problem occurs frequently when only artificial light is available – for example in factory foors which are lit by green-tinged neon light. These lighting situations appear flat and insipid and make it almost impossible to take an interesting photo. It has proven helpful to replace the lights, that is, to use daylight tube lighting instead of neon to deal with this problem. To create a vivid colour effect, it is only necessary to replace only every second tube. This creates an alternation of light colour and brightness in the image and conveys an impression of three-dimensionality and depth. Furthermore, as in every mixed light situation, there is the option to filter, use flash units or correct the colours in digital post-processing.

Generally speaking, when using artificial light, the images that work best are those in which natural daylight is simulated. Instead of the sun, a primary artificial light source is set up behind the camera. Shadows created by this primary light are brightened with small lights or reflectors placed to the side. Other lights are used as spots to emphasise surfaces or details. Artificial light which comes into the image through an open door or gap in a wall creates an impression of liveliness and depth.

Walls which extend into the room and also pillars can be detached from the background by positioning a light or a flash behind them. This prevents the pillar or the wall and the background merging into a featureless area of grey. When using either stationary or a mobile light, you should use an exposure meter and test shots to determine how powerful each light source needs to be or how often the flash needs to be set off. When using artificial light for an outside assignment, you should take extension cables, cable drums, fuses, replacement bulbs and a tripod for each flash with you.

If you frequently encounter problems with light, then deliberately train your eye to appreciate the effect it has. In any event, experience plays a particularly big part in positioning and measuring out additional light.

← Typical mixed-light photo with daylight and artificial light with several colours. Some corrective filtering was undertaken to even out the colours.

→ The strong neon light is the reason why this photo has green tinge despite the use of a filter when it was taken.

→ That is why the colours had to be corrected in post-processing to achieve a natural effect.

165 CHAPTER 4: PHOTOGRAPHIC PRACTICE

(4.3) — EXPOSURE METERING

The correct exposure is a prerequisite for a good photograph. Modern camera systems, both analogue and digital, offer features which appear to make an external exposure meter superfluous: these include LCD displays, histograms, or test photos with instant film, but primarily internal exposure meters employing various measurement methods. However, the ideal way to achieve the correct exposure is to measure the light – which is impossible with an integrated exposure meter. Therefore, exposure metering and control should always be carried out manually for architectural photos. This is because only spot metering is possible with an exposure meter integrated in the camera or the digital back.

Spot metering measures the brightness of the light reflected by the subject. Because it is based on an average brightness value, the exposures can be incorrect if the subjects are brighter or darker than average. Photos taken in snow are classic examples: they are almost always under-exposed when an internal exposure meter is used.

However, this error does not occur with light metering. This is because this method does not measure the brightness of the light reflected off the snow, but the brightness of the light hitting the snow. In practice, it is not possible to avoid taking light meter readings at several positions around the room, particularly at the lightest and the darkest places. This determines whether the dynamic range is manageable, or whether it will be necessary to use light or bouncers.

For external photos, it is necessary to wait until the position of the sun permits the shot to be taken. For example, to photograph a house façade in bright sunshine, the light is measured where the sun shines on it directly and also in the building entrance, which is shaded by a porch, for instance. If the dynamic range is too large, one either waits until the sun has changed position so that it is possible to manage the difference in brightness between the façade and the entrance, or one takes the photograph on a cloudy day. If it is not possible to wait for or create ideal conditions, then it is preferable to ensure detail in the highlights and accept that the shadows will have none.

The most accurate types of spot metering are multizone metering with an integrated exposure meter and multizone metering with an external spot meter. When a spot meter is used, the brightest and the darkest parts of the subject and a section of average brightness are measured. An average is calculated from these values and set on the camera.

This exposure method is fundamentally inferior to light metering, but frequently the only practical option for external architectural photography.

→ All the lights in the room have been switched on here and all the side doors opened to allow light in. Furthermore, there is indirect light from a flash to the left at the rear and from the side rooms.

→ A light meter for precision spot metering

↓ An exposure meter for light and spot metering

↘ Colormaster 3 F colour temperature meter from Gossen

(4.4) — THE RAW FORMAT

The rules governing white balance and colour temperature hold true for both analogue and digital photography. In digital photography, it is important that the data supplied by the sensor are stored in the camera in RAW format. With JPEG and TIFF, the contrast, depth of colour, white balance and other parameters which the photographer sets on the camera before the image is captured are applied to the raw data supplied by the sensor immediately after the image capture and before storage on the internal memory chip. The purpose of this is to reduce the amount of data. On the other hand, if you set your digital back to RAW format, all the sensor data are stored unchanged on the chip. This ensures that the whole range of options is available when post-processing and guarantees the highest quality images; the parameters set on the camera are not applied to the raw data immediately but stored as "tags" with the sensor data. This makes it possible to modify them subsequently without any losses. Using the RAW format therefore leaves considerably more scope for image processing than do the other formats. When an image is captured in RAW format, only the exposure settings, that is, the ISO value, the aperture and the shutter speed cannot be changed.

Unlike the JPEG or TIFF formats, for instance, this file format is not standardised, but differs from manufacturer to manufacturer and even from camera model to camera model from the same manufacturer. For this reason, manufacturers supply software with their cameras which can read and process the RAW files their cameras produce. For example, the Danish company Phase One supplies the software Capture One with their digital backs for view cameras. It can be used to process the RAW files from these backs. The converter Capture One 5 PRO is available at a higher price and can be used to process the RAW formats from manufacturers such as Canon and Nikon.

Other manufacturers have RAW converters for their software developed and marketed by hardware and software companies, with whose programs it is possible to process RAW files from the cameras of almost every manufacturer. Adobe, for example, offers Camera RAW, Apple the Aperture 2 program and Canon supplies Digital Photo Professional. The most widely used is Adobe's converter, Camera RAW, because it is available as a plug-in for Photoshop.

Once the most important settings have been made on the RAW converter – particularly the colour, brightness, dynamic range and clarity – the image data are stored in the TIFF standard format which can be read into every readily available image processing program. In order to allow the result to be reproduced or corrected, it is important to note the selected settings and to save the RAW file. Generally speaking, image data should be provided to customers, printers and designers in TIFF format, in the RGB colour space with 16 bit colour depth and 300 dpi. When output on DIN A4, for example, this resolution means a file size of around 45 megabytes.

Anyone who has acquired some experience working with RAW converters will not need HDR, even when wide dynamic ranges require managing. This is particularly advantageous when it is important to reproduce colours and contrasts as naturally as possible. The effect of images from RAW files is considerably more natural than the frequently hyper-real appearance of HDR photos (see section 2.10 High dynamic range imaging). However, in the long term, both the RAW format with its options and HDR will change the way people see because both technologies permit much more detail in highlights and shadow than is possible with analogue equipment and than one is used to seeing.

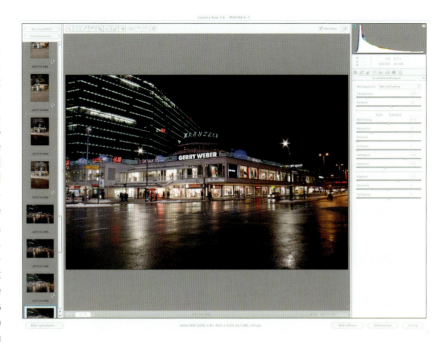

→ A screenshot of the RAW converter from Adobe

Chapter 5
Composition

Axel Hausberg/Anton Simons

173 Subject
173 Camera viewpoint, angle of view and distance from the subject
173 Focal length
178 Aperture and depth of field
178 Image formats
178 Foreground, middle distance and background
179 The Golden Ratio
179 The art of using lines

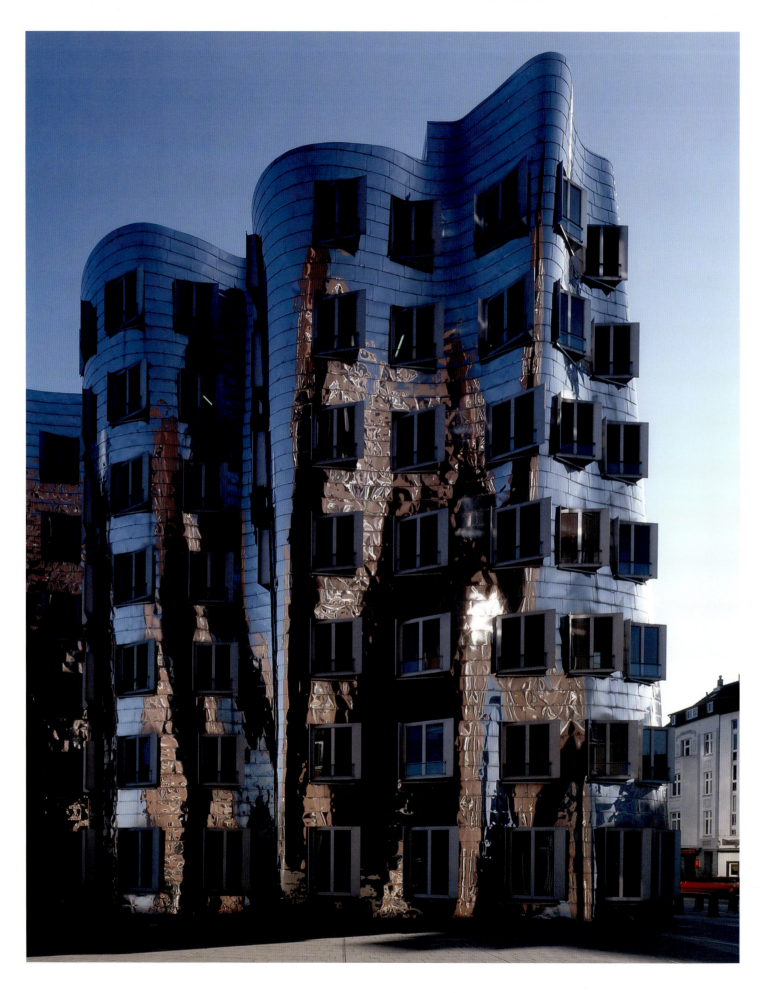

→ The easiest way to obtain a neutral point of view is to take the picture from approximately eye level and using a lens with the standard focal length.

← The photographer of architecture should be aware before taking the picture that this building from Frank O. Gehry is not a purely functional building.

Each photograph is determined by its subject, the way in which it has been exposed, the place from which it had been taken, hence the angle of view, and the distance from the camera, apart from the focal length of the chosen lens, the aperture and the picture format. Composition means influencing these parameters in a very specific way with the aim of producing a desired effect in the picture.

(5.1) —— SUBJECT

If the subject itself is either very original or spectacular, then as a rule it is very easy for the photographer to take a photograph that is original, good or noteworthy. In such cases it is the task of the photographer to decide on a location, a focal length and a format that capture the originality of the subject in the best possible way.

(5.2) —— CAMERA VIEWPOINT, ANGLE OF VIEW AND DISTANCE FROM THE SUBJECT

The easiest way to obtain a neutral point of view is to take the picture from approximately eye level and using a lens with the standard focal length. In this way you enable the viewer to look at the subject. A perspective such as this raises the object, making it look more massive and substantial. By choosing a low viewpoint you can, for example, emphasise the height of a high-rise building and lend a monumental effect to a squat and compact building. A low viewpoint also usually has the effect that the building that is photographed is emphasised within its surroundings.

However, viewpoints from a low level are counterproductive if it is a matter of making clear that a building fits in well with its surroundings. Often the best way to show this is to use a slightly elevated camera viewpoint. Such angles of view give the viewer an overview and help to clarify the incorporation of a structure into its context. The higher the selected viewpoint, the less familiar the perspective is for the viewer and the harder it is for him or her to recognise the building that is depicted.

If you photograph a skyscraper from a viewpoint that is close to the ground and correct the converging lines, this often produces the impression that the building is increasing in girth towards the top. For that reason the effect produced by a picture of a building is often better if it is photographed from a high viewpoint, either from another tall building in the vicinity or even from a helicopter. Viewpoints that are high up often give the viewer an impression of distance and spaciousness; sometimes they also give the feeling that the world is at your feet.

(5.3) —— FOCAL LENGTH

The use of a wide-angle lens also increases the impression of depth and vastness and also the dynamism of a structure. A telephoto lens brings closer

→ Here a perspective was chosen that plays with shapes in an abstract way.

→ The low viewpoint of the photographer makes this building look especially massive.

→ The combination of a low position when taking the shot and a wide-angle lens makes the viewer look up at the subject, in this case the Skytower in Frankfurt.

→ A slightly higher camera viewpoint makes clearer the integration of buildings into their context.

← If you photograph a skyscraper from a viewpoint that is close to the ground and correct the converging lines, this can produce the impression that the building is increasing in girth towards the top.

together buildings that in reality are far apart. In addition, pictures taken with longer focal lengths have a flatter and calmer effect (see section 2.1 Lenses and focal lengths).

(5.4) —— **APERTURE AND DEPTH OF FIELD**

A building can be picked out against its surroundings or the attention of the viewer can be drawn specifically to the façade or another element of the building if the photographer decides to use a wide aperture and so reduce the depth of field. Sometimes the depth of field is still greater than desired even with the aperture fully opened. This has the result that such areas are still shown sharply even though they should have disappeared into the unsharp part. In such cases it is possible to restrict the sharpness specifically to the desired area by applying the Scheimpflug rule (see section 2.13 on the Scheimpflug principle).

(5.5) —— **IMAGE FORMATS**

Another important element in composition is the choice of format. However, in many cases the format is dictated by the purpose. For example, many publications exclusively make use of portrait format title photographs. The number of columns plays an important part when it comes to illustrating texts in the inside. When using a two-column layout, two portrait pictures placed next to one another usually take up half a page. On the other hand, in a three-column layout a single two-column portrait picture takes up nearly two thirds of a page. In general, there are a number of tried and tested rules governing choice of format:

→ The most commonly used format is landscape format, presumably because it comes the closest to our own field of view. Landscape formats often have a calmer and more static effect than portrait formats. On the other hand, you can create a greater degree of asymmetry with them than with portrait formats. Landscape formats are of special importance for architectural photography if the building is to be shown within its surroundings.

→ Portrait formats have a more original, unusual and dynamic effect than landscape format photographs. For that reason also portrait format is the first choice for a whole series of subjects that constantly recur in architectural photography; for example, for towers, façades that are generally oriented vertically, and in all cases where the height of the building is to be emphasised. Furthermore, portrait format is very suitable for subjects that are split up into foreground, middle distance and background and where it is important to provide a sense of spatial depth.

→ Square picture formats have the advantage that you do not need to rotate the camera or the film cassette or the back to take the picture. Square photographs often give an impression of being calm, balanced, harmonious and self-contained. They have a feeling of compactness about them, often also a sense of being monumental. However, these formats tend to be seldom used in architectural photography. However, they should certainly be taken into consideration and especially when photographing subjects with a clear geometric structure.

→ Panoramic pictures with architectural subjects are extremely rare. The reason for that is due to the print media and the subjects. Panoramic pictures only work effectively in portrait format magazines if they are printed as a double spread over two pages. Extreme landscape formats with a page ratio of more than 3:1 are good for skylines; moderate landscape format panoramas with page ratios of up to 3:1 are suitable for pulling exceptionally long buildings out of their context. There are also isolated panoramic pictures in portrait format that are used to visually encompass a tower or another form of tall building.

The number of picture formats that are available is theoretically unlimited. For that reason you should feel perfectly free to break away from the standard formats of the camera and paper makers if it improves the composition and choose a format that fully matches the subject and the idea behind the picture. It is advisable not to compose the picture too tightly when taking the photograph so that detailed corrections can still be made later.

(5.6) —— **FOREGROUND, MIDDLE DISTANCE AND BACKGROUND**

Splitting subjects into foreground, middle distance and background is one of the rules that each visual artist gets to know right at the start if his or her training. Breaking up the pictures into three planes guides the eye of the viewer from the edge of the picture into the centre and this produces the impression that it is three-dimensional. This splitting into three planes is suitable for both portrait and landscape format pictures; but, it usually makes a stronger effect when using portrait format pictures. However, it is not always possible to divide the picture into three planes, as when photographing façades, for example.

Often it is a matter of making clear the embedding of a building into its surroundings. A harmonic splitting up into foreground, middle distance and background very frequently leads to imposing photographs. This applies to the same extent for interior shots: there the splitting up of the subject into three planes gives the picture a sense of depth. But it is also still possible to take impressive pictures if you flout this rule. The result then is abstract and two-dimensional pictures that are completely reduced to no more than areas, colours and shapes and allow the viewer almost no spatial orientation at all. The gaze and the attention of the viewer are almost fixed to such pictures due to the intense desire to find spatial orientation. However, such photographs are not really suitable for documenting interior architecture and serve better as advertising and art pictures.

(5.7) —— THE GOLDEN RATIO

A further important rule of thumb for picture layout is known as the Golden Ratio. This design rule is deeply engrained in our viewing habits and in our culture, it is often called the Rule of Thirds in photography, and has been taught to young painters, sculptors and other visual artists for centuries. This rule is based on the experience that pictures and other works of art whose main element is in the centre of a photograph are always at risk of appearing boring.

The Golden Ratio is therefore a design principle for an asymmetrical picture layout. This principle states that you should split up the picture area into thirds, both horizontally and vertically, so that you have a total of nine rectangles of equal size. According to the Golden Ratio the main element of the subject should be placed in the upper or lower horizontal and at the right-hand or left-hand vertical line. The main elements in architectural photographs can be a house entrance, a window or even a shadow. The only thing that matters is that they stand out from their surroundings. But use the Golden Ratio in the same way as all design and layout rules; do not simply follow it slavishly all the time. It is not infrequently the case that a truly eye-catching picture works precisely because it ignores this rule.

(5.8) —— THE ART OF USING LINES

Make use of prominent lines in the subject when composing a picture through a conscious use of lines. Edges are often used in interior shots, those from room ceilings or floors and walls. Lines like these that stretch out and provide depth can be used to simulate a three-dimensional effect, but also to draw the eye of the viewer to single points that are important within the picture or even to multiple points one after another.

But a conscious use of lines can also be employed to bring in a sense of disorder and confusion. A recommended way to check the effect of lines in a photograph is to close one eye and to squeeze the other until all the details disappear and the subject is reduced to its main structures. If two dominant lines cross at one of the four points of the Rule of Thirds then in one single picture you have followed both the rules of the conscious use of lines and also those of the Golden Ratio.

→ Wide-angle lenses convey an impression of depth, vastness and dynamism. Telephoto lenses, on the other hand, squeeze together buildings that in reality are far way apart.

→ This landscape format photo has a calm and balanced effect through the use of horizontal and vertical lines.

→ The asymmetrical layout of this picture gives this landscape format a sense of dynamism.

← A split into foreground, middle distance and background gives a sense of depth.

→ This picture has also been split into three, with foreground, middle distance and background.

→ Square photographs often give an impression of being calm, balanced, harmonious and self-contained.

→ This extreme panorama gives an overview of the buildings in the harbour.

→ This moderate panorama pulls the building out of its surroundings.

→ This 120-degree view was taken with a panorama camera.

→ The split into foreground, middle distance and background gives a spatial feeling.

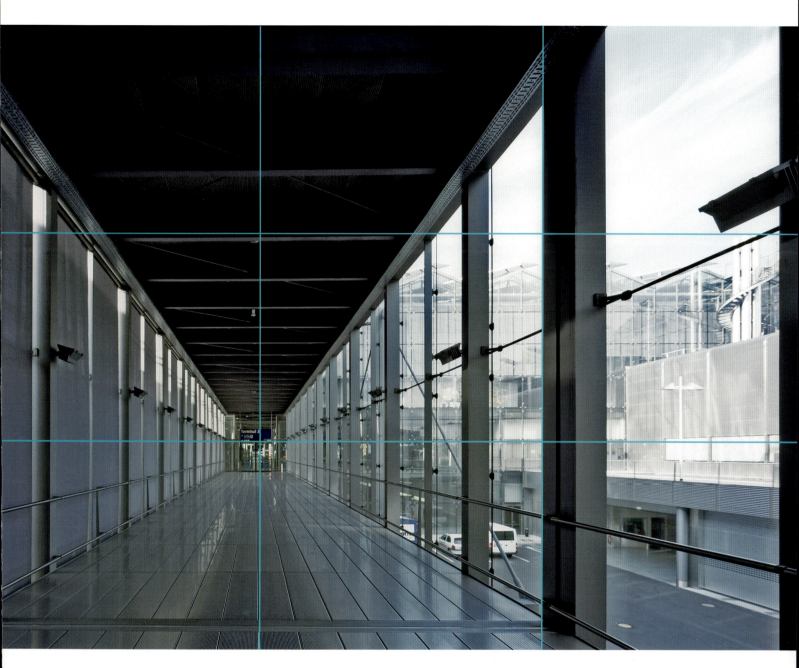

→ This picture was composed in strict accordance with the rule of the Golden Ratio.

← This views plays with areas and shapes; there is almost no sense at all of three-dimensional depth.

→ The lines of the roof structure direct the eye of the viewer to the check-in counter.

→ Here the diagonals in this photograph make it feel dynamic and lend it depth in a case where the main subject is dominated by horizontal and vertical lines.

→ This picture is self-contained despite the confusing multiplicity of lines.

→ The lines of this central perspective drawn the eye to the exit.

Chapter 6
Post-processing

Axel Hausberg/Anton Simons

196 Developing
197 Scanning
199 Image editing
208 Finishing

Developments in photo technology have led to the profession of photographer repeatedly changing to a greater or lesser degree over the years. At the very beginning the photographer himself stirred the emulsion that he then applied to negative plates made of glass to coat them. After the exposure he developed the plates and produced contact prints all by himself, once again using photographic paper and developer that he had made himself. Only later were photographic plates and – somewhat later still – film produced on an industrial basis so that the photographer could concentrate more than previously on the actual handwork. Since plates, films, laboratory chemicals and photographic paper were all standardized, it was comparatively easy to master the subsequent laboratory work.

When Agfa brought colour films onto the market in 1936, followed a little later by Kodak, many professional photographers gave up developing their films and the production of enlargements and had both these jobs done by a photographic laboratory. This was because the laboratory work had to be carried out in absolute darkness, unlike for black-and-white materials, the temperature tolerances were significantly tighter than those for black-and-white photography, and the filtering to be applied when making enlargements was a completely new topic in itself that was barely possible to master in addition to the actual photographing. The profession of photofinishing laboratory technician came into being. The digitisation of exposure technology and post-editing has meant that the post-processing is increasingly being done again by the photographer. This is primarily due to these three reasons:

1. <u>Increasing prices and pressure of time.</u>

2. <u>The hardware and software that are required for professional image editing are affordable nowadays.</u>

3. <u>Today professional image editing programs offer so many and relatively easy options for retouching, error correction, optimisation and control over the colour, contrast and brightness plus composition that it is now well worthwhile editing your own image data.</u>

Photographers from all the sub-disciplines therefore work digitally throughout, all the way from the exposure to the finished photograph. However, a great many architecture photographers still use analogue film, as they did before, and for several good reasons:

→ Digital technical cameras are extremely expensive. In particular, digital backs are hardly affordable for the novice.

→ There is a huge quantity of top-quality analogue cameras, lenses and accessories available on the second-hand market, and at relatively affordable prices. The development of lenses for technical cameras lags behind the development of digital backs because in all cases the lens makers can only start with the development of new lenses when a new sensor chip comes onto the market.

→ To date digital technical cameras have offered notably fewer adjustment options than do analogue solutions; this is a problem above all in the wide-angle range for architecture photographers (see section 3.3 The view camera).

→ Many photographers who have been working with the 4×5 inch ground glass screen for many years or even decades regard the change to a screen or a display with a size of only 53.99 millimetres × 40.49 millimetres as a massive step backwards. In any case, the screen and display at the digital back are more than 80 per cent smaller than the analogue ground glass screen that they are used to.

→ In the pre-digital era the purchase of this specialist equipment was regarded as being once and for all, for the rest of your professional life. That has changed radically in recent years. There will be huge progress in the development of backs and lenses for technical cameras in the next five to ten years.
For that reason it is highly possible that the digital equipment that you buy today will be technically out of date in just a few years. Many architecture photographers are therefore postponing the decision to buy digital equipment into the indefinite future and scan their slides and negatives so that they can edit them digitally afterwards.

(6.1) —— **DEVELOPING**

Just as before, there are numerous photographers who do not develop their negative and slide films themselves but instead leave that work to a processing laboratory. However, the number and density of such laboratories have diminished in recent years. Today you can only find processing laboratories in a few big towns, and most of them only work with certain materials and formats. For that reason you should find out well in advance which laboratory in your area offers which services, what they cost and how quickly the services can be provided.

Since photographers generally work with laboratories on a long-term basis, you should find out about how easy the laboratory is to reach and if parking is available nearby. In practice it is often advisable to bring the exposed material personally to the laboratory – often on the way back from a photo shoot. Alternatively, a courier service can be used to pick up the finished work.

If you wish to be independent of external service providers, or if that is in fact necessary, then you have to develop your own negative and slide films. First of all, you need to acquire the requisite knowledge, and then invest in a developing machine and a drying cabinet. Above all, you need a room that can be used as a darkroom. In addition, there are the ongoing costs for the developing and fixing baths. The procedures and costs for disposal of the chemicals vary from area to area; you can obtain information from the communal or municipal refuse collection centre.

(6.2) — SCANNING

Scanners are the indispensable link between the worlds of analogue and digital photography. Cleanliness is the non plus ultra when it comes to working with a scanner. For that reason photos, and especially film, must be cleaned very carefully before scanning to remove dust and marks. This can also be done by editing on the computer, but it takes a great deal of time. Always wear lint-free cotton gloves when handling negatives and slides, and these can be obtained from photo and computer shops. In the meantime there are now also antistatic gloves that prevent the film material from becoming electrically charged when it is touched. The material to be scanned is best cleaned with an antistatic dusting brush, which is available with and without a blower. The glass parts of the scanner can be cleaned with an antistatic fluid and cleaning cloths that are available from photo shops. After the work is finished, always keep the scanner closed so that no dust can settle on it. A good way to reduce the concentration of dust in the air in the room is to use an air conditioner.

Before scanning, in the scanning program you select the image size, resolution, colour depth and tonal range by choosing a file format. The settings that you choose depend in the first instance on the intended purpose. The resolution of a scanner is specified dots per inch (dpi), (1 inch = 2.54 centimetres). This number is the basis for measuring the degree of precision with which scanners, for example, but also cameras and other optical devices, scan a subject or a photograph, positive or negative. The resolution capability of an optical device is described by the maximum resolution that this device can achieve. The image size and resolution are directly linked to one another. The photographer should first find out from his client how big the desired picture is to be when it is printed later or whether it is to be used on the Internet. The scanner setting for the resolution can then be derived on the basis of the principle "as high as necessary, as low as possible". However, always allow a certain amount in reserve in any case. A resolution of at least 300 dpi is required to achieve a high-quality printout. On the other hand, 72 dpi is sufficient to show an image on a computer screen.

The greater the colour depth of a scan, the more differentiated the colours are when printed. Set a colour depth of at least 16 bit to avoid colour artefacts in the photo later. A TIFF file for a photo in DIN A4 format has a size of around 45 megabytes for 16 bit colour depth and a resolution of 300 dpi.

Special care is needed when setting the tonal scale. What is meant by the tonal value of a picture is the number of gradations between the lightest and the darkest points of the picture. Since a maximum of 256 tones is possible in the PostScript format, the standard output format for typesetters in the graphics business, it is possible to display 256 grey tones and with the three basic colours 256^3, or 16.8 million, colours. With the histogram function the tonal range of the picture to be scanned can be shifted to within these so that the colours can be made lighter or darker. The range between the lightest and the darkest points in the picture can be spread out or reduced by using the contrast setting. When scanning photographs it is usually a matter of reproducing many tonal value gradations and hence as many details as possible. In addition, the subjects should be shown with as much contrast as possible; on the other hand, it is important to take care that there is detail in both the lightest and the darkest areas of the picture. The task is therefore to find a balanced relationship between contrast and brightness when setting the scanner.

Today many scanning programs offer an automatic function that first measures the brightness values for the white point, hence the lightest pixel in the picture, and the black point, hence the darkest pixel. The program then sets the level of brightness to an average value that it determines from these two values. Finally, the automatic mechanism raises the contrast until the brightness value is zero for the black point and the white point reaches brightness value 255. However, automatic functions only give satisfactory results for subjects with an even distribution of brightness. It is necessary to make manual corrections for subjects in which light or dark areas predominate.

Many scanning programs also allow you to set the black and white points manually. If a spot exposure meter was used when the picture was taken the black and white points can be set at the same points when scanning as those used for the original exposure. All the pixels that are lighter than the white point and

→ Colour artefacts occurred in the sky during scanning or subsequent editing.

darker than the black point are cut off by the scanner. The tonal range that lies in between is stretched. You should adhere to the following rules when setting the scanner:

→ Set the white point in a light part of the picture with a neutral colour in which details are still preserved. With architectural subjects placing the white point in windows or clouds is a good choice. This point and all lighter areas in the picture will later be shown as white.

→ Set the black point in a part of the picture that is almost black but in which details are still just visible; in architectural photography this is often the night sky, asphalt surfaces or slate in shadow. This point and all darker parts of the picture are rendered as black later.

→ The black and white points should always be placed in areas of the picture with a neutral colour, otherwise there is a risk of creating colour artefacts. Pictures of interiors that were taken under artificial lighting or with mixed lighting often do not have any areas with a neutral colour. In such cases a grey scale wedge helps: once you have placed it on the glass plate next to the picture to be scanned, the black and white points are set on this grey scale.

→ Architectural pictures taken in fog or mist often have neither a black point nor a white point. High-key pictures taken with backlighting sometimes do not have a black point. The grey scale wedge helps here as well.

→ As opposed to the JPEG format, the TIFF format works without compression and losses. This ensures maximum quality in scanning and subsequent editing. It is also used so widely that just about all image editing programs can read and edit it. The disadvantage of this format is that the files it produces are relatively large.

(6.3) —— IMAGE EDITING

The actual post-production starts after the scanning. In analogue photography errors are corrected by filtering during the exposure or later in the laboratory, and finally in the enlargement. There are more options when editing images on the computer. However, an evaluation of the picture must be made before it is edited. For that reason the brightness and contrast, the effect of the colours and the sharpness are checked one after another and corrected as required.

Brightness and contrast
When checking the brightness and contrast, ensure that the highlights and shadows still show some detail. If that is not the case, then more minor errors can be corrected with the image editing program. If the errors are too marked then the scan must be repeated. Reduce the contrast so that the error is not repeated. If necessary, the brightness could also be corrected upwards or downwards. If it turns out that the scanner is not in a position to digitise the pictures such that the image of the original cannot be reproduced properly, then the only answer is to find a more capable scanner. The basic principle is that the contrast must be set to be relatively soft rather than too hard. At the prepress stage there is always the option to change the contrast to match the image file optimally to the printing machinery.

Colour
Look for colour casts when checking the colour. It is not always possible to completely eliminate colour casts at the time of taking the picture through white balancing or filtering. In addition, it is always the case that a slight colour cast is intensified by the scanning process. However, each colour can be tweaked individually by modern image editing programs so as to make it lighter or darker, weaker or stronger. These options mean that removing colour casts is no longer a problem. It is also possible to get control over mixed lighting situations through the options provided by digital image editing, while on the other hand problems with mixed lighting involve compromises when using analogue laboratory methods. The reproduction errors that are typical for digital photography – image noise, moiré effects and chromatic aberration – can likewise be removed with digital post-processing or at least toned down to an acceptable degree. When checking the colours using slides and prints that act as a reference, this should always be done under standard lighting conditions. If a grey scale chart was photographed at the same time with the subject, then click on this card on the screen to define the neutral grey.

Histograms
Histograms are a further aid for evaluating the raw data of pictures and to correct the contrast, gamma and brightness values when editing the image. They illustrate graphically the frequency of the individual tones that occur in a picture.

The value for black (zero) is entered on the far left and the value for white (255) on the far right. The values for the grey levels (1 to 254) can be read off between these extreme values.

The histogram of a photograph can provide hints on how and how much a picture can be corrected by editing. If the main part of the histogram is as shown in the graph of the histogram on the left, then the picture

→ Picture information was lost here because the contrast settings were overdone.

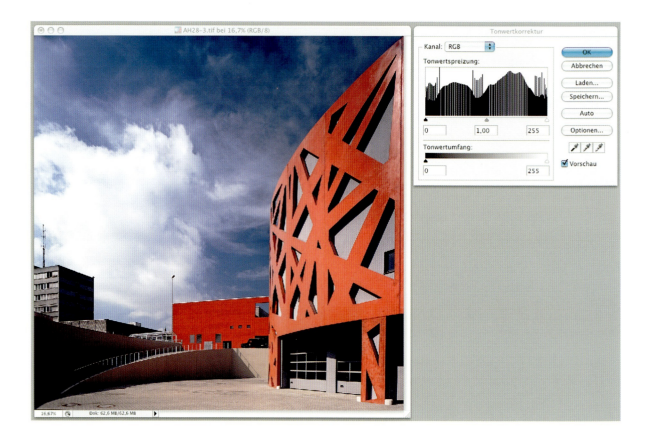

→ Here the histogram curve does not have any gaps.

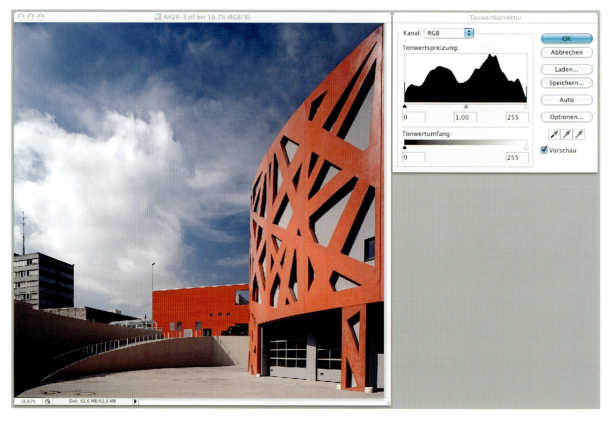

is dominated by dark tones. That might have been what the photographer wanted, but it is also possible that the photograph is under-exposed. If the main part of the histogram is as shown in the graph of the histogram on the right, then light tones predominate. This can also be an indication of over-exposure. Optimally exposed photographs often exhibit a Gaussian bell curve whose highest point is somewhere in the middle.

When carrying out post-processing you should not shift the tonal values of the picture to be edited too far either to the left or to the right, nor should you push them too much into the middle, otherwise there is a risk of losing picture information. If the brightness distribution is regulated in the post-processing solely on the basis of a histogram and not also with regard to the subject and the statement that the picture is making, there is also the risk that the pictures will lose their individual character and so appear lifeless and artificial. Aim in the first instance for a natural effect when tweaking the contrast, gamma and brightness values of a picture; the histogram should only be used to provide a starting point; there is no one histogram that is optimal for all pictures. Proceed cautiously and work "by eye" when setting the values. Good intermediate results should be saved as a TIFF file.

If a histogram shows gaps at certain brightness levels this can be an indication of colour or brightness artefacts or other errors. Since errors of this type cannot be corrected by editing, the original must be scanned again or even a new photograph taken.

Retouching
If a grey scale chart had been photographed as well, this can also be edited out in the same way as other unwanted elements: roads signs, cars and bicycles, graffiti, damage to the building and broken window panes together with dustbins, animals and branches that intrude on the subject can all be removed. Last of all, any dust particles and scratches from the scanning can be removed.

Rotation and perspective correction
The correction of horizontal and vertical converging lines is not as important in any other photographic discipline as in architectural photography. Before undertaking any perspective or objective corrections you should bring up a grid to check if the picture was properly aligned. Even if the picture had been taken with the aid of a spirit level and ground glass screen and the photograph had been correctly placed on the glass area of the scanner, it is still possible that minor corrections in the clockwise or anticlockwise directions will be necessary.

Modern image editing programs provide the option to make perspective corrections at the post-processing stage, but a number of disadvantages must be taken into account if this function is used:

1. If corrections are made horizontally then the building looks squatter, and thinner if corrected vertically. Admittedly, image editing programs such as Adobe Photoshop give the option to extend in both length and width objects that had been squeezed down vertically so as to restore the actual relationships of the sides. Apart from the photographer's own subjective impression there is no visual starting point. It is only possible to reconstruct the actual side relationships of a building by measuring if it was photographed from the front. However, this presupposes that you know the dimensions of the building.

2. The edges become fuzzy if perspective corrections are made. Furthermore, this creates a lack of sharpness that is not distributed evenly over the picture. It is possible to correct for this within certain limits. However, you should always avoid any lack of sharpness because it creates an unnatural impression.

There are still photographers who believe that it is not necessary to use the camera adjustments and movements now that it is possible to correct trapezoid distortion, or converging lines, digitally in an image editing program. However, that is a major error: correcting trapezoids to rectangles on the computer results in the ratio of the subject width to the subject height becoming incorrect. In addition, correcting the distortion requires interpolation, in which the image editing program inserts additional pixels into the picture. However, this is only possible at the expense of sharpness; furthermore, in structures with more contrast it produces colour fringing. Image processing programs actually incorporate algorithms to suppress colour fringes; this likewise reduces the sharpness even further.

The following applies. If the photograph is taken with the correct movements and shifts this saves a subsequent time-consuming correction of the perspective with an image editing program; above all, it is not necessary to take into account any loss in sharpness and irritating colour fringing.

Furthermore, you can even decide at the time of taking the picture whether you need to change the location of the camera if you are to include all of the subject and without any converging lines. However, if you only discover later on the computer that the framing of the subject was too tight to allow the

→ This picture of the abbey of Maria Laach was taken with a special camera with vertical movements. The proportions are reproduced true to life.

→ This picture was taken with a camera that was set up parallel and without using any movements.

→ This picture was taken from the same viewpoint with the camera tilted upwards.

→ In this digital perspective correction the original image has been stretched upwards. This makes the building look more compressed than it really is.

→ In this digital perspective correction the original image has been squeezed together downwards. This makes the building look thinner than it really is.

→ Picture made with the camera tilted upwards

→ Display in the image editing program after the perspective correction

→ Uncorrected version with the grid shown in the image editing program

→ Complete corrected image before cropping

→ After cropping

→ No additional sharpening was done here.

→ The subject here was sharpened too much in the image editing.

→ If distortion is corrected then colour fringing and a lack of sharpness appears at the edges, as this enlargement shows.

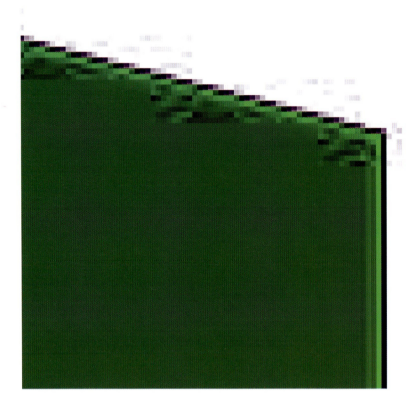

distortion to be corrected completely at the monitor, there is no other choice but to repeat the shot.

For that reason converging lines should always be corrected when taking the picture if at all possible and the image editing program should be reserved solely for fine-tuning. However, it is not always possible to completely avoid converging lines when taking the picture. Sometimes local circumstances dictate the use of viewpoints for the picture that are so close to the building to be photographed that the options and movements on the camera are not sufficient for full correction when taking the picture. This is the case in particular in big cities when photographing skyscrapers that are close to one another. In that case you should:

1. look for a place from which to take the picture that is the best possible from the point of view of perspective correction.

2. make full use of the adjustment options of your camera.

3. correct any remaining problems on the computer.

However, you need room to correct horizontally converging lines on the computer – especially at the top edge of the picture. You should bear this in mind when taking the picture. The way to check if a photograph exhibits converging lines is to superimpose a grid and check whether the horizontal and vertical lines are parallel. If that is not the case, then corrections must be made.

Further corrections and cropping

Next, pay attention to possible vignetting and chromatic aberration. Such errors cannot always be avoided even when using high-quality lenses. Strong shifting almost inevitably means that there will be vignetting in the corners. However, professional image editing programs offer the option to remove vignetting by lightening the corners. The picture should then be viewed on the monitor with high magnification. If green or magenta colour fringing can be seen at sharp edges, then it is a matter of chromatic aberration that can likewise be removed with a suitable program. This also applies to image noise and moiré effects and to barrel and pincushion distortion. The picture is cropped right at the end (see section 5.5 Image formats).

(6.4) —— FINISHING

Paper is after all the oldest medium for photographs. However, today an ever greater proportion of photographs exists in the form of bits and bytes on hard disks, DVDs and servers. Nonetheless, there is one thing that still holds true, and that is the fact that photographs only give their maximum value and effect on paper. This applies to an even greater extent in architectural photography. A photograph on paper also has the unbeatable advantage that it is an object with an existence of its own as opposed to the volatility of an image on a monitor. For that reason there is no getting around the requirement to produce the photograph on paper when it comes to applying for orders or for display in exhibitions and presentations. In the same way as the paper, the frame for the picture also contributes a considerable part to the overall impression that is created by the photograph. Just like the paper that is used, a frame can add value to a photograph – or take it away. For that reason it is important to devote sufficient attention to the selection of a photo frame and not to reduce the power of the statement made by the photo by using a frame of lower quality. Cheap frames often make the picture look cheap as well.

Media materials

Since the demand for photographic papers for analogue enlargements in the processing laboratory keeps dropping, the number of manufacturers and the selection available keep shrinking. Makers such as Agfa, Orwo and Argenta, who were virtually synonymous with photography for decades, have given up the production of paper or have even disappeared completely. By contrast, it is hardly possible any more to get an overview of the selection of papers available for printing. In 1983 Ilford was the first company to introduce a multigrade paper that allowed a wide range of gradations of hardness to be produced from just one grade of paper. This British invention quickly dominated the market and reduced to a niche segment papers with a fixed gradation, for which there had previously been no alternative. The most common materials for analogue and digital photos are baryta papers, cotton cellulose and polyethylene which are available in glossy and matt finish and with all kinds of surface structures.

Modern materials and technologies, especially digital printing, which has largely displaced silk screen printing, make it possible, or at least easier, to print photos on a wide variety of materials and also make it more cost-effective – for example, on fabric and sheets made of plastic, on metal, glass, tiles and other ceramic materials. The durability and colour accuracy of photos on various substrate materials have likewise improved dramatically. For a number of years now it has even been possible to print photos for outdoor hoardings onto washable plastic fabrics. This has also opened up new possibilities for photographic art in construction.

→ When producing an application folder, glossy papers are recommended, just as before – above all, because the colours appear the most saturated. An attractive option when advertising yourself as an architectural photographer to potential clients are photo-books that are now being offered by many service providers. These books are also available in panorama formats in sizes of up to 30 by 40 centimetres and with high-quality bindings. Since photo-books are relatively inexpensive, it is not a serious problem if they get lost or damaged when being sent to or from a customer, for example.

→ As before, the standard material for exhibition photos is baryta paper. This material, which can be archived, conveys a sense of timeless value. Presumably that is the reason why it is preferred by most collectors and art devotees. Nonetheless, it can still be well worthwhile to occasionally print photos that are intended for exhibition onto unusual materials as well – photographic linen, glass or metal. This not infrequently gives the photograph a special effect; it also provides a means to make it stand out from its competitors.

→ In order to be able to show what is possible, every architecture photographer who has enough space to do so should build up a collection of those of his photographs that were exceptionally successful, printed on unusual materials as well.

Once you have made a few test runs printing pictures on unusual materials you will see that one and the same subject can have a quite different effect when printed on various materials. But not just the photograph itself and its intended purpose should form the basis for a decision in favour of or against a particular material, but also the client's taste, the surroundings in which the photograph is to be permanently hung or exhibited, plus the size of the room, its lighting and style of furnishing.

Framing

The range of frames on offer is truly huge. Generally speaking, picture carriers should be distinguished from picture frames. Picture carriers are primarily used to stretch photos that have been enlarged or printed on photographic linen or some other fabric. The most cost-effective are stretch frames made of wood. The photograph is first stapled to this frame and then stretched and permanently fixed by means of small wedges.

In addition, there are also stretch frames made of aluminium, likewise for photos printed on woven materials, and these can be reused several times. The picture is fixed in place by clamping it with a rubber lip in the frame. Due to the thickness of the material,

→ Not only the perspective had to be corrected when the picture was taken, but further amendments had to be made during the digital post-processing in this shot of skyscrapers in Frankfurt.

→ The camera was shifted horizontally to the left for this picture (indirect parallel shift). For that reason the parallel-running horizontal lines of the building have been reproduced as parallel as well.

→ This photograph of the same subject was taken from the same viewpoint without any camera movements.

→ Here the previous picture has been subjected to digital perspective correction.

→ The proportions have been falsified due to the digital perspective correction.

→ Photographs that are intended for exhibitions should also be printed on unusual materials if the occasion warrants it.

→ Reusable wooden frames were adopted for this photo exhibition.

→ Big enlargements are being used increasingly for advertising purposes and for art in construction.

→ This aluminium stretch frame can be reused several times.

the picture carrier that is invisible to the viewer gives the impression of making the picture stand out from the wall or partition. This gives the photograph depth and turns it into an object. The big disadvantage of these carriers is that they do not protect the picture, against dust and contact, for example.

Picture frames fulfil the task of placing a photograph in its surroundings. For that reason you should not only consider the photograph but also its background and its surroundings when choosing the frame.

Picture frames can likewise be divided into two large groups: permanent and clip-on frames. Clip-on frames are only intended to hold the photos for a relatively short time. For that reason they are primarily used for exhibitions that will only be held for a limited length of time. Every professional photographer of architecture should have a set of such frames to use for exhibitions in galleries or in his own studio. In terms of design, such frames should be restrained and capable of being used in many different ways. The main problem when framing is to get the glass and the picture completely free of dust.

It is best to make the choice of a permanent frame together with the buyer. Only he or she knows in what surroundings their photo is to be viewed. Good permanent frames have the advantage that they allow a photo to be sealed off against air and dust and thus can last a long time.

→ When using wooden stretch frames the pictures are stapled to the back.

Passe-partouts are often used as the mediating element between the photo and the frame. The cutting of a passe-partout can be left to a framing service, which can usually be found in every larger town. If you wish to do the cutting yourself, you require a cutter that is available in various forms and price ranges. Passe-partout card is – just like photographic paper – available in assorted colours and thicknesses and with various surface finishes. It is largely a matter of taste for a particular colour, surface structure, thickness and width. The basic principle is this: the bigger the picture, the thicker and wider the card. And the thicker the card, the greater the impression of depth. A thickness of two to three millimetres has been proven to be best when using clip-on frames.

Anyone who invites visitors to changing exhibitions in his own studio has virtually no alternative but to invest in a gallery rail system. Such systems allow various forms of hanging with different picture heights and widths.

The lighting also makes a big difference to the overall impression that the viewer has of a photograph. Here it is recommended that a light source with as neutral a colour as possible is chosen.

Archiving

Sleeves made of glassine, acetate and polyester are available for the archiving of pictures, negatives and slides. They can then be stored together with their sleeves either hanging or placed flat in folders or cardboard boxes that must be made of acid-free buffered materials. Special cabinets made of metal, plastic and wood are available for the archiving of folders and boxes. When buying it is advisable to check that the material of which the cabinet is made does not give off any harmful gases that could cause damage. The archiving room must be dust-free, dark and consistently cool and dry as far as possible.

Negatives and slides are best sorted chronologically and then numbered. Here each day should start with the number one, and each year should have a folder of its own. Make an overview for each year that is kept as a cover sheet together with photographs, negatives or slides. This overview should make it possible to quickly tell which client you worked for and which subject you photographed. The same applies to negatives and slides as for files, namely, do not archive everything but only the material that is genuinely usable.

Image files should always be archived in RAW format, and edited files in TIFF format as well. In order to structure the data it is recommended that you create year folders with day sub-folders on the data medium that is used. Archiving programs offer the option of adding keywords to images so that they can be found again in the database simply by searching for keywords.

Today there are hard disks with a storage capacity in the region of terabytes that have enough space for an entire "working life as photographer". RAID systems are suitable for data backup; they consist of multiple hard disks on which the data are mirrored automatically. Losses from theft or fire, for example, can be avoided by also saving the data onto CD-ROM (from 650 megabytes), DVD (from 4.7 gigabytes) or Blue-Ray (from 25 gigabytes) and keeping the media in a bank safety deposit box or other secure place. The data media should be carefully labelled beforehand. Use a permanent marker to write directly on the data media or onto labels that are to be stuck onto the data media. Note that there are enormous differences in the quality of digital data media. The fact that quality cannot be assured even when buying well-known reputable brands does not make it any easier to buy the right ones. Data media should also be stored in dark and dry conditions and away from dust. Duke boxes are recommended for all those who use CD's and DVD's not only for long-term archiving but also for daily use. For example, the Imation Disc Stakka CD/DVD archiving system that can be connected via USB offers space for 100 disks.

Since digital data media also age, it is advisable to regularly copy your own data onto new data media. The copied files should then be compared against the original files to be absolutely safe.

Pictures should be archived in folding passe-partouts that are suitable for long-term storage. Fingerprints always leave grease and acids on the picture surface and these damage the pictures over the long term. For that reason you should always wear thin cotton gloves when working with pictures so as to avoid any direct contact with the photographs. However, it does not harm the picture if you occasionally touch its passe-partout with your bare hands. In addition, you can quickly frame together with the passe-partouts pictures that are stored with passe-partouts. If you do not use passe-partouts then put spacer sheets between the individual photographs so that they do not touch one another.

Since photographs are of various sizes and formats, each photographer needs to find out for themselves whether it is best to file their pictures by format, chronologically, thematically or by client. Usually a combination of the various filing systems is best. Each photograph on paper should be labelled in such a way that the corresponding negative, slide or original image file can be found quickly if required. Photographs can be marked on the back or in the white edge at the front below the actual picture, preferably with a soft pencil.

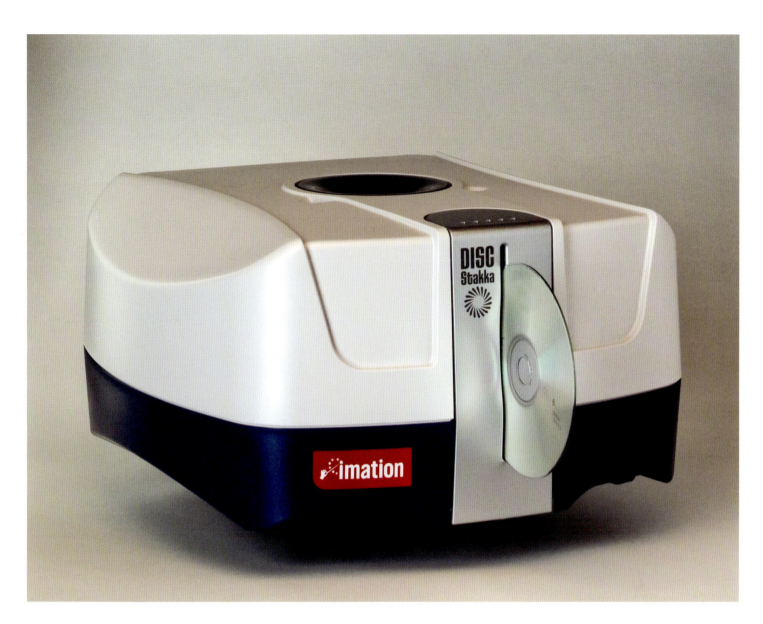

→ Imation Disc Stakka CD/DVD archiving system with space for 100 disks and which can be connected via USB

Chapter 7
Colour management

Axel Hausberg/Anton Simons

224 Camera calibration
225 Calibration of the development process
225 Monitor calibration
228 Scanner calibration
228 Printer calibration

The shapes, details and structures of buildings must be reproduced to appear as they are in reality – that is what architectural photography is all about. A no less important role is played by the reproduction of the colour values as they were in the original, and the same applies for the density, brightness and brilliance of the colours. However, evaluating the colours and predicting the results that will come out of the printer is, as previously, still a problem in digital image processing. Professional photographers do not leave colour reproduction either to chance or to a purely subjective impression. The various measures to be taken to ensure the reproduction of colours as they are in reality can be summarised under the term colour management. Colour management also serves the purpose of making use of the entire colour space that the equipment for taking and outputting the picture can provide. A further effect of deciding on colour management is a reduction in costs: it is a matter of reducing waste to a minimum.

The most important thing to be done in colour management is to match up with one another all the components that are used to take, process and output pictures. This is the only way to ensure, for example, that the slate grey of the façade of a new building can be reproduced in an advertising brochure so that it looks true to life and is without any falsification. If the original and the picture do not match up there may even be contractual problems in such cases.

The matching up of the equipment, the software and the work sequences is called calibration. It is of equal importance in analogue and digital photography. The makers of film material and monitors do of course pay great attention to a constant colour reproduction of their products. Even so, it is impossible to avoid slight production variations. Furthermore, monitors, films and laboratory chemicals are subject to aging processes. And, at the end of it all, each photographer has to put together individually their equipment for the processing of his or her images from the wide variety of hardware and software offered by the various makers. For that reason he must calibrate all their items of equipment separately – everything from the camera to the printer – if they want to be sure of getting reproducible colour results.

Many vendors have been making great efforts for many years now to develop automatic colour management systems. They are intended to save the photographer the task of calibration – even when they are used with a collection of equipment whose individual items have not been matched up with one another by the maker. However, until now it has only been possible to calibrate optical systems fully automatically. Photographers with a claim to being professionals must therefore calibrate their systems by themselves, just as before, if they place any value on predictable results and consistently high quality in image editing. Even so, colour management systems can provide help in such cases.

The following items of equipment are matched up with one another in calibration:

→ Camera with lenses
→ Development of negatives and slides
→ Scanner
→ Monitor
→ Printer

In essence, the calibration process has the aim of leaving the original data of the image unaltered and only modifying the output at the monitor and the printer through colour filtering.

(7.1) —— **CAMERA CALIBRATION**

Colour management starts even before the picture has been taken: in analogue photography this is done by choosing the right film, and in digital photography by using the white balance function. In analogue photography you use daylight film in daylight and artificial light film when working under artificial light. Alternatively, you can work exclusively with either daylight film or artificial light film and apply the corresponding colour filter as required. Calibration is especially important for shots of interiors with artificial or mixed lighting because the lamps have very different colour temperatures, but it is almost impossible to assess this with the human eye. There are four options for calibrating cameras, of which only the first two are possible with analogue cameras while all four procedures are possible with digital cameras:

1. Determine the prevailing colour temperature with the aid of a colour temperature meter. From this value the device automatically calculates the filtering that is required to produce a photograph that gives the impression that it has been taken in neutral daylight with a colour temperature of around 5,500 degrees Kelvin. Anyone working with this method must have on hand a minimum set of colour correction filters.

2. You can also use a grey scale chart as a cost-effective alternative to a colour temperature meter: Place it somewhere within the subject that is to have neutral lighting in the photograph and photograph it as well. During the post-processing on the computer the card is defined as a neutral grey point and finally retouched out.

→ Grey scale chart

→ iColor Display 3 from Quatographic is a product for monitor calibration.

3. If the camera has been set for automatic white balance, then it automatically performs the white balancing routine before each picture, in the same way as with multi-field autofocus and multi-field exposure measurement. This will in fact adequately handle the vast majority of exposure situations. However, in terms of accuracy it does not approach that which can be achieved with manual white balancing.

4. In order to carry out manual white balancing, at the location and under the requisite lighting conditions hold a grey scale card or white card a short distance in front of the camera lens so that only the card can be seen in the viewfinder. Then indicate to the camera in the way described in the user instructions that the colour value of this card corresponds to 5,500 degrees Kelvin.

(7.2) — CALIBRATION OF THE DEVELOPMENT PROCESS

The next step is colour-neutral developing. If you develop your own films that is no alternative to calibrating your own developing process. This is done by making a test series with the laboratory chemicals of your choice and your own equipment. This starts with photographing a standard colour chart, preferably under reproducible studio conditions. As an alternative, the colour chart can be photographed under indirect daylight. Then develop the film according to the maker's instructions. After drying, slide film can be compared on a standardised light table against a standard colour chart. If negative film is being used, it is first necessary to make a standardised positive. If the slide film or the positive does not reproduce the colours true to the original, then the pH value of the film chemicals must be adjusted in accordance with the maker's instructions.

Of course you can only work with this calibration as long as you use the same film, the same laboratory chemicals, a constant throughput speed and the same temperatures. Furthermore, consistent results are only possible with a developing machine. If you move the film cartridge by hand you will always find unexpected colour changes later. If you switch to another type of film or different chemicals, such as those from another manufacturer, the process has to be calibrated all over again. Anyone wishing to send their films to a processing laboratory for development should, before choosing a particular laboratory, expose a number of films identically, then send one to each of the various processing laboratories for development and then compare the results. In general, you should only send your films to certified laboratories.

(7.3) — MONITOR CALIBRATION

The most important item of hardware for the evaluation and editing of colour is the computer monitor. The photographer must be able to evaluate on the screen the changes that he or she makes with the program while editing the image. Monitors for professional-level image editing must be capable of displaying the entire RGB colour space, and hence nearly all photographers, graphic designers, service providers and printers work with them. However, only a few monitors from specialised manufacturers have this ability, which is crucial for ensuring that the colours are reproduced correctly when subsequently printed. The monitors are relatively expensive, but there is no getting around this investment if colour accuracy is important. Tube-type monitors must be switched on for at least half an hour before calibration and before any editing that requires truly accurate colours so as to reach their operating temperature.

→ The left-hand photo, that has been digitised with a calibrated scanner, reproduces the actual colours without any falsification. The scanner had not been calibrated before the second photo was digitised.

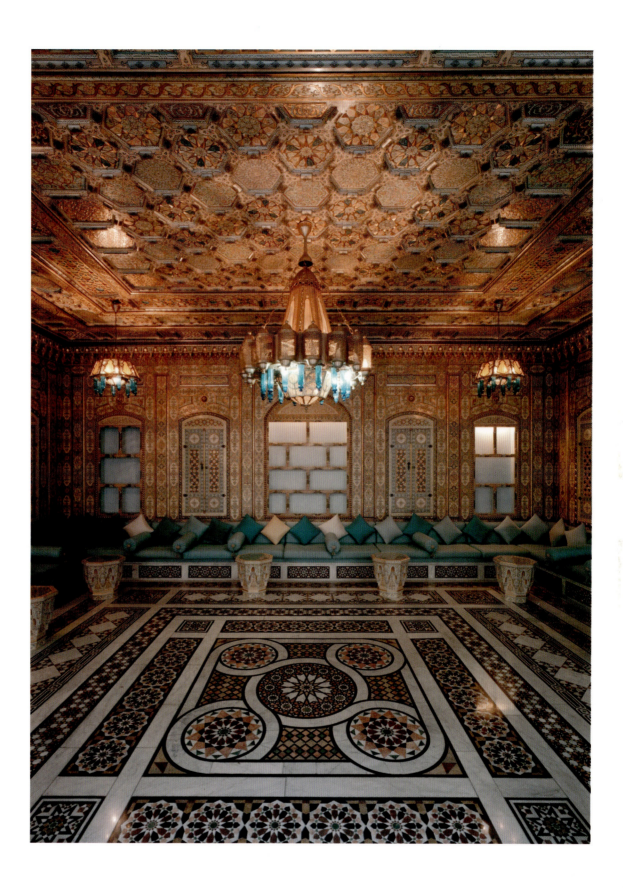

227 CHAPTER 7: **COLOUR MANAGEMENT**

Only then is it possible to be sure that the colours will not change any longer. The lighting should always be the same in the calibration.

The calibration of the monitor is done using the program supplied by the maker and this matches the monitor to the operating system of the computer and the image editing program that is used. For the calibration you simply follow the step-by-step instructions in the program. This calibration software mostly provides sufficient accuracy of colour. However, this does not reach the accuracy of hardware calibration.

A colorimeter is required for calibration by using hardware. This device, which looks rather like a computer mouse, is hung in front of the monitor or attached to it with a suction cup. The photocell in the colorimeter measures the values of the colours that are displayed by the monitor. These values are then compared against standardised colour values. The program then creates from the difference a correction profile, the values for brightness and contrast, for the primary colours of red, green and blue, for the gamma value and grey balance as well as the black value. Once these correction values have been confirmed the program automatically applies this correction profile to each image file that is displayed on the monitor.

(7.4) — SCANNER CALIBRATION

Each scanner has its own colour characteristics. Not only the units of each individual scanner manufacturers but also the units of one and the same manufacturer do not uniformly interpret the colours of the photographs that have been digitised with them. For example, some scanners work with green in the highlights but with magenta in the shadows. And there are even noticeable differences between the scanners of one type or model. Professionals work with calibrated scanners to compensate for these differences. As with monitors, so for scanners; not every single model that is available is necessarily adequate for professional use. For that reason there are drum scanners for use by photographers and digital service providers for the digitisation of negative and slide films; however, such devices are very costly. In addition, significantly cheaper flatbed scanners are also available with which both reflective and transmissive scans can be made and so meet professional requirements.

Scanners are calibrated with software tools; there is no hardware calibration for scanners. This is done by first scanning in a standardised template for colour checking (IT-8 template) that matches the film material that is to be digitised later. Ensure that the template and the reference data in the program come from the same maker. After scanning, the program compares the setpoint data against the scan and calculates a correction profile from it that is then applied to all scans and serves as a digital filter to correct colour casts. A separate profile must be created for each type of film used. Even with the most careful calibration, a cheap scanner can never reach the resolution, density and differentiated reproduction of colours and structures that is possible with a top-end unit.

(7.5) — PRINTER CALIBRATION

If you do not provide pictures on paper for your clients but only supply image files, or if your photos are printed out by a suitable service provider, then you can save the investment in a proof printer. However, if you make the printouts for your clients yourself, then the purchase of a photo-printer of this type is recommended. However, these printers, which are mostly inkjet printers, must also be calibrated. There are programs for this which guide the user through the calibration process and need to be worked through step by step.

A calibrated scanner and a calibrated monitor are required for printer calibration. First of all, a reference template is scanned in, which is supplied by the maker of the program to enable printer calibration. This file is then printed out on the printer to be calibrated and measured with a colorimeter. The program then compares the measured data against a reference file and calculates from it a correction profile that is then applied to each printout.

This profile only applies to a particular printer-ink-paper combination. If you work with several types of paper then a separate correction profile is required for each combination. In the meantime paper makers offer correction profiles for each type of paper they make and for all current types of printers, downloadable free of charge from the Internet.

Good results can be achieved with these ready-made files that save the photographer from doing their own hardware proofing. However, for top precision it is still necessary to do your own calibration.

Once the entire chain from the camera to the printer has been calibrated, print out several test files and compare them under standardised lighting conditions with a colour temperature of 5,500 degrees Kelvin against the monitor display and, if applicable, against the original slides.

If necessary, you can now carry out the fine-tuning and correct any colour shifts.

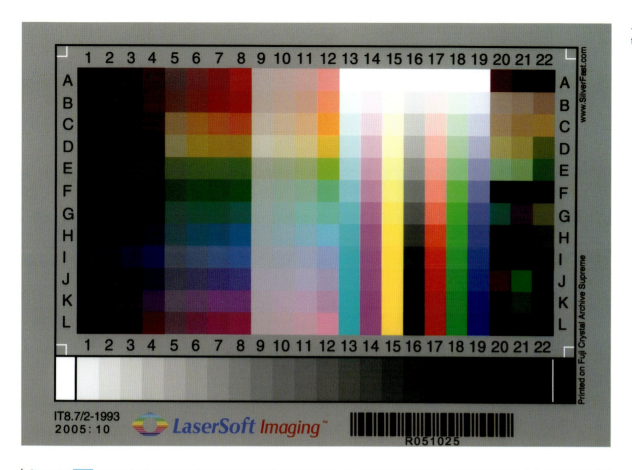

→ The IT-8 template from LaserSoft Imaging

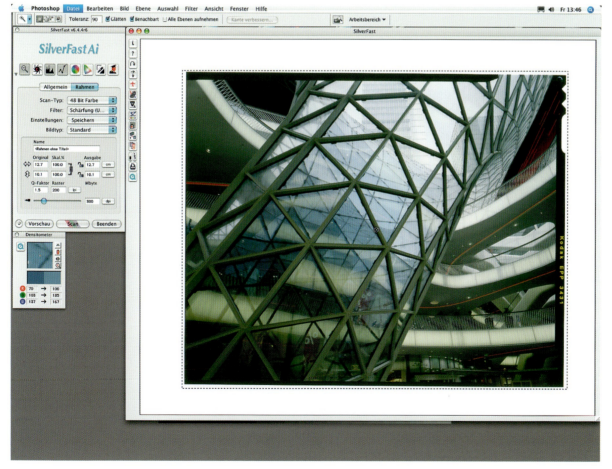

→ Dialog window of the scanning program SilverFast Ai

Calibration is only useful if the defined ambient conditions remain the same. These conditions include above all standardised lighting conditions when working at the monitor and when evaluating images of slides and printouts at the illuminated table. Since all the devices along the production chain age, it is necessary to recalibrate the individual components at regular intervals:

→ The camera white balance routine should be run before each individual picture.

→ The laboratory process should be checked every time the film chemicals are changed.

→ The monitor should be checked on a monthly basis.

→ The scanner should be tested twice a year.

→ Printers should likewise be checked twice a year. However, the test intervals should be shorter if the printers are used heavily.

→ Scan of a 4 × 5 inches slide in its original size.

Chapter 8
Composition and artificial worlds, model photography, photogrammetry

Axel Hausberg/Anton Simons

234 Computer-generated imaging
234 Photogrammetry
234 Model photography

→ This artificially generated high-rise block has been integrated into a photograph.

Anyone taking a close look on the Internet at images from photo-communities and microstock agencies can see that many architectural photos are not simply retouched. They have actually been enhanced with blue skies, velvet lawns or other decorative elements which have been cut out of other photographs. This is where retouching crosses over into collage or composing.

(8.1) —— COMPUTER-GENERATED IMAGING

Computer generated imaging (CGI) takes this one step further. Photographs are no longer composed from actually photographed elements but are generated entirely on the computer. Like the transition from retouching to composing, the transition from composing to CGI is seamless. CGI software enables perfect images of buildings, building complexes and whole districts to be generated artificially even before they have been built. This technology lets architects and urban planners present realistic images of their planned buildings to clients at the tendering and competing stage.

Such computer-generated images are often used after construction too, for instance for brochures, Internet advertising and for record purposes. CGI images are not only produced for buildings which do not (as yet) exist but also for existing buildings and historic architecture.

(8.2) —— PHOTOGRAMMETRY

However, the new opportunities for generating artificial worlds do not render photography superfluous since photographs are frequently used as the basis for the manufacture of CGIs. The underlying data for images of historic or other old buildings for which no longer exists any building documentation are not provided by the architect. They are constructed from several photographs taken of the building. These computer-generated technical drawings are referred to as photograms. Photogrammetry is the non-contact remote sensing and surveying of buildings, site formations, miniature models or other three-dimensional objects on the basis of photographs. Photogrammetry is used to define the spatial location or the three-dimensional form of the subject matter.

Use is frequently made of this relatively recent development prior to undertaking renovation projects if the construction plans for historic buildings, building complexes or whole districts are no longer available, or if such buildings are to be reconstructed in miniature form. For a photogram, the objects to be surveyed are photographed from several perspectives consecutively. These photographs used to be taken

using special survey cameras. Since software is now available that can calculate construction plans from photos however, these special cameras are no longer required. In fact computer programs can now reconstruct buildings from ruins.

(8.3) —— MODEL PHOTOGRAPHY

Before it was possible to generate images of planned buildings for tenders, exhibitions, presentations and competitions on the computer, miniature scale models

→ This representation has been entirely computer-generated.

were often made of the planned buildings. These models have the advantage that they can be viewed in three dimensions from all sides and that they provide a realistic impression of proportions, height ratios and spatial relationships. Architectural models are also often seen in museums where, for instance, they show what a city looked like in earlier times.

Architectural models are either produced by the architecture office itself or are commissioned from model makers. These models are frequently reduced to the simplest structures and made of card, wood or polystyrene – either piece by piece by hand or by CNC-machining from a single block of material.

Highly detailed models are also manufactured from several material, for example, from metal, glass and plastics, with a very high degree of detail accuracy. Models are generally divided into the following types:

→ Cutaway models refer to models in which sections of buildings are cut away like slices of cake in order to allow viewers to see inside.

→ This image was also generated on a computer.

→ Functional models are those in which buildings are, for instance, lit from the inside or have moving doors.

→ Models are referred to as stacked when it is possible to remove individual storeys from buildings in order to see inside.

→ Planning studies are those which show only the broad outlines of buildings and omit details.

→ Massing models are models depicting not just a single building but a whole settlement, district, village or entire city.

→ Detail models are of parts of a building, for instance one room, rather than the whole building.

Frequently, however, photographs were and are also taken of architectural models. Model photography falls into the grey area between architectural and product photography. Photographing models of buildings requires all the knowledge and experience of architectural photography, particularly in the handling of form, colour and materials. However, it also requires special expertise and product photography equipment. Professional model photographers require a photographic studio with flash equipment including spotlights, studio spots and light shapers which are designed to light even miniature models precisely. Macro lenses are required because the lens and the object are very close together in model photography and these are not part of the standard equipment of the architectural photographer. Some model photographers also work with endoscopy cameras or attachments.

Clients for CGIs and models are usually architectural and urban planning offices, property developers, estate agents, investors, local authorities and exhibition venue builders.

→ Photograph of a functional model

→ A model of Berlin before the Second World War

238

→ Photograph of a cutaway model with a view into the rooms of the penthouse apartments

→ This photograph of the interior of a model was taken with an endoscopy camera

→ 1:200 scale draft model for the Loews Hotel Monte Carlo from 1976. At this time, models were still produced completely by hand with no PC, CNC milling or cutting plotters.

Chapter 9
Equipment tips

Axel Hausberg / Anton Simons

244 Cameras
244 Lenses
245 Flash equipment
248 Accessories
248 Developing equipment
248 Computers and monitors
248 Scanner and scanning software
249 Printers
249 Image processing software

Digital photography and the Internet are the reasons why photography techniques and the job of the photographer have undergone such far-reaching changes in just a few years. Architectural photography is the only photographic discipline in which analogue technology still plays a serious role. However, there can be no doubt that the future of architectural photography is also digital.

(9.1) —— CAMERAS

Anyone (initially) wanting to explore the world of architectural photography with a digital small-format camera should make sure that the camera's sensor chip is full-frame, that means measuring 24 × 36 millimetres. This means maximum resolution and minimal noise and moiré. In addition, it is, only way to fully exploit the focal lengths of the extreme wide-angle lenses. The half-frame (APS-C) actually extends the focal length of these lenses by a factor of more than 1.5. Basically, cameras for architectural photography should permit time exposures which allow the attachment of a timer or cable release. They should support the RAW format, allow the superimposing of a grid and be equipped with an attachment for a circular level or spirit level. Canon and Nikon supply bodies as well as the largest selection of lenses and shift lenses. Schneider supplies shift lenses for Canon and Nikon camera bodies as well as for Minolta, Pentax and Leica bodies.

Medium-format

The number of manufacturers of medium-format cameras has fallen steadily in recent years. The choice in this range is therefore relatively small. Mamiya supplies shift lenses for its cameras and there is a shift adapter for Hasselblad cameras. Cameras from both these manufacturers can be used as either analogue or digital cameras with the corresponding back.

View cameras

The greatest available choice is in view cameras with the trend decreasing in the analogue range and increasing in the digital sector. The manufacturers are working feverishly to develop digital cameras, backs and lenses. It is therefore hard to know whether service, consumables and accessories will still be available in five to ten years for the cameras and adaptations which are current now.

Newcomers to analogue view photography are recommended to buy a second-hand 4 × 5 inch, or 6 × 9 centimetre format camera on an optical bench which has ideally been factory overhauled. There are plenty of materials and accessories available for these two widespread formats. The 4 × 5 inch format is the largest and is therefore the format with the most detailed reproduction and the highest resolution. Thanks to the lenses available for this standard format it is also extremely suitable for wide-angle work. There is also a wide range of accessories for this type of camera.

Newcomers to digital photography are recommended to buy a 6 × 9 centimetre camera either on an optical base or XY concept. XY cameras have neither bellows nor optical bench. This type of camera allows continuous horizontal (X-axis) and vertical (Y-axis) adjustment. The distance between the image and the lens standard, however, is invariable. In the traditional view camera both the image and the lens standards can be varied. The distance between the image and the lens standards is also variable. The scope for horizontal and vertical shifting and for tilting and pivoting is also less with the XY camera than for the view camera with optical bench. XY cameras are, however, very light and compact. Since they can be very precisely adjusted, they are a particularly attractive option for digital photography. XY cameras are hardly ever available on the second-hand market.

Notable view camera manufacturers are Linhof, Arca-Swiss, Sinar, Cambo, Horseman, Alpa and Plaubel. The current view camera models are designed for both analogue and digital use. Either the camera manufacturers themselves or the digital back manufacturers supply adapters with which digital backs can be used. Four digital back systems are currently in production from Phase one, Leaf, Hasselblad and Sinar.

(9.2) —— LENSES

The basic equipment of the architectural photographer, whether working with a small-format or a view camera and whether analogue or digital, is as follows:

→ An extreme wide-angle lens with a focal length corresponding to a small picture format of 20 millimetres or less.

→ A wide-angle lens with a focal length corresponding to the 35-millimetre small picture format.

→ A standard lens with a focal length corresponding to a small picture format of 50 millimetres.

→ A medium telephoto lens with a focal length corresponding to a small picture format of 70 to 100 millimetres.

→ An actual telephoto lens with a focal length corresponding to a small picture format of 200 millimetres.

If you only buy one lens when you start out you should choose the wide-angle lens as this is the most frequently required focal length. The second lens most frequently used by architectural photographers is the extreme wide-angle. You can always crop wide-angle pictures to look like a normal or even short telescopic range lens but you cannot do the reverse.

When buying a lens the rule is to buy top quality. It is always better to buy a single high quality lens rather than two cheap ones. Analogue photographers using small-format or view cameras need not necessarily buy the latest generation lenses. The Schneider/Kreuznach and Linos/Rodenstock websites still include information about view lenses which have been out of production for years. Nikon, Zeiss and Fuji have stopped production of view lenses but with a little luck, it is possible to find reasonably priced high-quality view lenses from these manufacturers on the second-hand market. Anyone buying a second-hand digital lens should ensure that the objective lens is in good condition, that the lenses are compensated, that the shutter works and particularly that the long shutters times are accurate.

When purchasing digital lenses you should always choose the most up-to-date to ensure that they will be compatible with the latest sensor generation in terms of sharpness, image quality and size. However, today digital view lenses are only made by Schneider/Kreuznach and Linos/Rodenstock. Zoom lenses are unsuitable for professional architectural photography because amongst other things they produce distortion errors which are almost impossible to correct on the computer afterwards. Shift lenses for small-format cameras are produced by Schneider, Canon, Nikon, Hartblei and Leica. Anyone thinking of buying this kind of lens should be aware that they are almost as dear as view lenses. Zörkendörfer supplies shift adapters for using medium-format lenses on small-format cameras. This kind of solution is only worthwhile if you already have medium-format lenses. In many larger towns and cities there are photographic shops which hire out lenses. This is a good way of testing out a lens before a possible purchase.

Photographers graduating from the analogue to the digital view camera can carry on using their analogue lenses under certain circumstances. There are no general answers, however, to the question of which analogue lenses can be used with which digital back. The only way to find out is by trying out each lens on the digital back of your choice. Retailers and manufacturers are aware of this issue and will lend out digital backs to try out. The most reliable test of whether an analogue lens fits a specific digital back is by the sharpness of the image. You should therefore compare several test photographs with printouts or on-screen representations of files taken with the lens and an analogue back.

Since the digital sensor is smaller than the conventional film formats for view cameras the focal lengths of analogue lenses will be extended. If, therefore, you combine old analogue lenses with a digital back, you will need to supplement your lenses in the wide-angle and extreme wide-angle range. In that case you should opt for digital lenses.

(9.3) —— FLASH EQUIPMENT

If you take indoor shots with a small-format camera you can use small-format system flash equipment for fill flash and as a mobile light source. The luminous power of these devices is generally around 100 Watt-seconds. At optimum lighting conditions these flash devices also suffice for minor fill flash when working with medium-format and view cameras. Professionals, however, need to purchase a studio flash system because the luminous power of small-format flashes is not sufficient to illuminate larger areas even when several are used together. There are two types of studio flash systems:

→ Compact flash units with a generator integrated into each flash head and

→ Systems in which generator and flash units are separate.

A system with three flash heads and least 500 watt-seconds is ideal. If you decide to buy a generator you should choose a device with least 2.500 watt-seconds. If you occasionally require more heads and more power, you can hire additional units from specialist dealers. Each flash head has a tripod and a set of filters included as standard. For light shaping you also need standard reflectors, auxiliary lamps, shields, honeycomb louvres, flap attachments and filter holders. Before buying a second-hand or a new flash system you should find out what is included and about servicing.

→ The Arca-Swiss Rm3d, an XY camera for analogue and digital backs

→ The Sinarback eMotion 75 LV – Sinar arTec XY camera with digital back

→ Digital lenses from Rodenstock's Gigaron S and Gigaron W series

(9.4) —— ACCESSORIES

The basic equipment of an architectural photographer along with the camera, lenses, digital or analogue back (in the case of 6×9 centimetre roll film) or sheet film holders (in the case of 4×5 inches format) and flash equipment is as follows:

→ a tripod and tripod head

→ a circular level or spirit level

→ a lens hood (compendium in case of view camera)

→ a cable release

→ a black cloth

→ normal and wide-angle bellows

→ a Fresnel lens

→ a magnifier for inspection

→ a blanket on which to lie if taking photographs from a low camera angle, on which to place camera equipment to avoid damage and with which to cover your equipment

→ a polarisation filter

→ a set of colour correction filters in cyan, yellow and magenta with which to filter out colour casts in artificial light

→ a neutral grey filter with a density corresponding to three to four stops, used to extend the exposure time to allow moving objects within the frame to be photographed without overexposing the image.
You also need:

→ an exposure meter

→ a colour exposure meter

→ a grey card

→ a folding ladder

→ a camera bag

→ a carry case

→ a carrying trolley.

You need to store a 4×5 inch camera in a sturdy carry case due to its size. A folding trolley is recommended for carrying the case and tripod. An alternative is a case with castors. These cases are large, heavy and awkward but have the advantage of being able to carry ladders as well. A folding ladder is essential to enable you to take photographs from higher camera angles.

(9.5) —— DEVELOPING EQUIPMENT

Anyone wanting to develop negative and positive film in laboratory trays needs to know that the results will vary in terms of colour, brightness and contrast because it is almost impossible to control temperature and processing times exactly. Therefore this type of developing should be left to the amateurs. Professionals should use drum developing equipment which is only manufactured these days by Jobo and Colenta. Processors from other manufacturers are available on the second-hand market. When buying you should make sure that the device has automatic temperature control, automatic filling and rinsing functions and automatic process time control. Laboratory chemicals are supplied by the manufacturers of the equipment and by Tetenal, Fujifilm and Kodak. You are advised to invest in a drying cupboard or a film dryer. These are available from, for instance Jobo and Kindermann.

(9.6) —— COMPUTERS AND MONITORS

Today both Apple and PC systems are supplied for professional image processing. When purchasing you should make sure that your system has sufficient RAM and that is compatible with the image processing software. When buying a monitor you must choose one that can be calibrated in terms both of software and hardware and which can display the full Adobe RGB colour spectrum. The screen should be 20 inches from corner to corner and should have a matt surface. Market leaders in this segment include Eizo (Color Graphic), Quatographic (Intelli Proof) and NEC (SpectraView).

(9.7) —— SCANNER AND SCANNING SOFTWARE

The choice of developing equipment has shrunk in recent years in the same way as that of negative and disc scanners for view camera formats. The market leaders are the X1 and X5 from Hasselblad. Both systems process film up to 10×24.5 centimetres and photos up to DIN A4 format. Alternatives are flatbed scanners with transmitted light – for example, from Epson (Perfection V750 Pro, Expression 10,000 XL) and Canon (CanoScan 8,800 F). This equipment, however, does not give the resolution or the quality of the Hasselblad scanner. For medium-format film Nikon offers the Super Coolscan 9,000. There are also attractive models on the second-hand market, for instance the Topas from Linotype which is no longer manufactured. When buying a used scanner you need to make sure that it has an interface that will connect to your computer and that it runs with your computer and software.

The required software is almost always supplied at no extra cost with scanners. New computers however are often no longer fitted with the SCSI interface needed by a scanner, nor do they support the drivers and software for older scanners. You can usually get round this problem by purchasing an SCSI card or SCSI/USB adapter and the professional scanning software Silverfast from LaserSoft Imaging (www.silverfast.com/de).

(9.8) — PRINTERS

A basic printer priced at around the 100 euros mark is ideal for producing quotes and invoices. Before buying a special photo printer, however, you should consider carefully whether you actually need this kind of device and whether it is worth investing in this kind of printer, which is around 1,000 euros for DIN-A3 format. Inkjet printers have become the standard in professional photo printing in recent years due to their unsurpassed quality, brightest colours and realistic prints.

The high costs of ink and paper mean, however, that prints from these printers are relatively expensive. If you have a good, reliable photographic services provider in your area you are well advised to have your prints done by them. You will save not only the outlay but also the costs of experimentation and regular recalibration of the printer plus maintenance, test prints, bad prints and rejects. You do get a degree of flexibility with your own photo printer which can be invaluable if a client needs prints at short notice.

Because photographic service providers operate on a larger scale they can buy their consumables relatively cheaply and offer their customers competitive prices. It is not always worthwhile, therefore, to buy your own printer.

If you do decide to buy one though, make sure that it can handle glossy as well as matt paper and that the inks are archive-proof. A professional architectural photographer should be able to deliver a format of at least 30×40 centimetres. Unfortunately, printer prices increase disproportionately as the format increases but at least the ink prices for larger printers are far lower than for small ones. Epson, Canon, Kodak and HP are amongst the leading manufacturers of photo printers.

(9.9) — IMAGE PROCESSING SOFTWARE

An image processing program for architectural photography must offer the following functions:

→ Brightness control

→ Contrast control

→ Colour correction

→ Resharpening

→ Vignette removal

→ Removal of noise and moiré

→ Correction of chromatic aberrations

→ Distortion correction

→ Rotation

→ Perspective correction

→ Cropping

If you choose a program without an integrated RAW converter and image management you need to compile your own program to do this. Adobe Photoshop has become the quasi standard for professional photographers in recent years. This program offers a wealth of functions but is relatively expensive and uses lots of memory. New entrants can choose from a range of significantly cheaper alternatives – for instance Adobe Photoshop Elements, Ulead Photo Impact and Corel Paintshop Pro. The very high-performance open source program GIMP is actually free to download from www.gimp.org. When purchasing, make sure that the software is compatible with your own computer system.

→ The ATL 1,500 drum processor from Jobo

→ The ATL 2,500 drum processor from Jobo

→ The Jobo Mistral film dryer

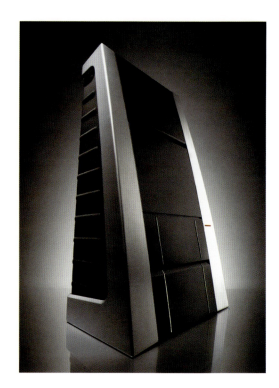

← The Flextight X5 is currently the top model amongst Hasselblad scanners.

→ The 24-inch CG241W monitor from Eizo is designed for image processing

← The Perfection V750 Pro flatbed scanner from Epson has a transparency unit.

→ The Stylus Photo 1,400 from Epson prints formats up to DIN-A4.

← The Expression 10,000XL von Epson scans documents up to DIN-A3 format.

→ The Stylus Pro 9450 model from Epson prints photos up to DIN-B0+ format (44 inches wide).

251 CHAPTER 9: EQUIPMENT TIPS

Chapter 10
Earning money from architectural photography

Axel Hausberg/Anton Simons

254 Pathways into architectural photography
256 Tax and insurance
256 Marketing
258 Quotations, calculations, offers and orders
259 Working with picture agencies
266 Photographic right in practice using five legal cases

It has never been easier to earn a little extra cash each month with architectural photos. Making a living from it has never been easy though and these days it is more difficult than ever. Only a very few get rich in this profession. To be successful as an architectural photographer you need a good training and several years, experience with the camera. And that is not all. You also need to think and act like a business person. These issues are addressed in this chapter.

First of all we talk about pathways into architectural photography from traditional training to the self-study route. This is followed by important information for those who want to become independent as professional photographers. This includes tax and insurance along with a range of legal issues from copyright to general business terms and conditions. We also address key skills including marketing and customer acquisition along with equally important issues such as picture fees, calculating prices and working with traditional and micro-stock agencies.

(10.1) —— PATHWAYS INTO ARCHITECTURAL PHOTOGRAPHY

The professional title of photographer is no longer legally protected (in Germany). For some time now anyone has been able to call themselves a photographer. For young talent this has the advantage that there are no institutional hurdles to overcome. The fact, however, that there are no conditions to meet before being entitled to call yourself a photographer means that it is hard for customers to tell the charlatans from the professionals.

Interns and assistants

The most common route into the profession of architectural photography is via an internship or as an assistant. An internship is an excellent opportunity to test out whether you are going to get enough from the work to make a career out of it. It can often be years before you can be sure which photographic discipline best suits you. In any case it makes sense not to settle for architectural photography immediately but to train in different genres and with different photographers before making your decision. Photographers have their own personal styles and foci. They have developed their views and working methods over the years and every photographer works with slightly different equipment.

Some architectural photographers are such purists that they will not allow humans or animals and often not even plants in their pictures. They focus exclusively on the pure forms, colours and materials of the architecture. Others see architecture as being made by humans for humans and people are therefore essential elements of their architectural photographs. For this group of photographers, buildings become subjects only when their interiors indicate that people live, work and communicate inside them. Photographers are also hugely divided when it comes to the question of added light. At one end of the scale there are the purists who work only with the existing natural and artificial light and who refuse to use any flash or additional lighting. At the other end of the scale stand photographers who believe that you should use any means possible to produce a better picture.

The Internet is the best place to research photographers who offer internships. Websites also give you an important first impression. Names and addresses of (German) photographers can also be obtained from the Bund der Freiberuflichen Fotodesigner, Centralverband Deutscher Berufsfotografen and from other photographic associations as well as from German Architects (www.german-architects.com) and other Internet forums. You usually apply for an internship by e-mail or letter. If you have received no reply after three weeks you should follow up your enquiry by telephone. If you get an internship and it lasts longer than three months you should insist on payment.

It is quite common for a photographic intern to be subsequently employed as an assistant. The job of the assistant is to take as much work as possible off the shoulders of the photographer and to carry out simple photographic assignments independently. You should use your time as an assistant primarily to learn. It is also recommended to collect samples of work and to start building up your own equipment. After any assistantship you should obtain written confirmation of the tasks with which you were entrusted, the equipment with which you worked and of the work you carried out. As well as employed assistants there are also freelance assistants, who provide services and are paid on a daily basis, earning around 200 euros per day.

Vocational training

Another means of entering the photographic profession is to undertake an apprenticeship via a vocational college and a master photographer. This kind of training lasts three years and concludes with an apprenticeship examination. It is divided into broad-based foundation training and specialisation in the third year. Interns choose to specialise in portrait photography, product photography, industrial and architectural photography or scientific photography. This new differentiation in the third year enables companies to match interns more easily to the available commercial pathways. In Germany the Centralverband

Deutscher Berufsfotografen provides information for those interested in finding out about companies which take on apprentices. Apprentice employers do include photographers who are not members of the Centralverband. Apprentices earn around 300 euros per month in their first year of the apprenticeship.

Regulated photographic training has the advantage over internships that the apprentice has three years of regular employment. The disadvantage is that apprentices are tied to a single employer for the duration of their training while the internship route offers experience in different studios and genres. Qualified apprentices who want to continue their professional development may, after five years as an apprentice, embark on a course for preparation for a Masters certificate. However, a Masters course costs around 7,000 euros.

An alternative to the vocational college/apprenticeship route is to attend a full-time course at one of the public or equivalent educational establishments. A list of such institutions is given in the appendix.

Study

The third option is to study photography at a public or private sector university or technical college. Access requirements are A-levels or equivalent qualifications. These institutions also have very varying educational goals and qualities. Therefore it is worth researching on the Internet before deciding on a particular course. You should ask questions of students, student associations and graduates and obtain information from independent advice centres. You should find out, for instance, whether the names of students of the particular institution regularly appear in award lists and whether graduates have succeeded in making a name for themselves as photographers. A list of names and web addresses of technical colleges and universities offering courses in photography is included in the appendix.

Self-study

On the face of it the most difficult route into professional architectural photography is the self-study route. Those choosing this path needs to ask themselves seriously whether they have the necessary discipline and staying power, never mind the requisite talent. All of this is essential if you intend to reach your goal by this path. Ultimately, photography enthusiasts working in another profession have no other option than to pursue the part-time self-study route. Nevertheless, there are plenty of examples of successful side-stepping into the photographic profession.

Self-study means that you work through specialist literature independently, that you find out about the latest developments by regularly reading the specialist press, that you spend weekends and holidays attending courses and that you participate frequently in relevant forums and other photo sites on the Internet. As a series of basic lectures, the German *Photokollegium* by Jost J. Marchesi is unsurpassed. This nine-volume work not only provides a complete foundation of photographic knowledge, it also suggests a wealth in practical exercises, something that is particularly important for independent students. In addition to pure photography, the independent student should systematically acquire basic knowledge in architecture, architectural styles and art history along with commercial knowledge.

Photographic courses are never cheap. However, a high price is no guarantee of course quality. To be on the safe side, you should either attend courses given by manufacturers or look for courses with a good reputation.

Anyone choosing the self-study route should follow up as many contacts and ideas as possible. It is a good idea to take part in photographic competitions and exhibitions and to visit trade fairs, museums and galleries as well as studying albums and taking part in online discussions in photo communities. It is also worthwhile starting to compile and maintain your own portfolio and to visit trade fairs and exhibitions to get people to look at your work.

Summary

Without an internship with one or preferably several experienced photographers, successful self-study is practically impossible. Even when you have learnt how to take good photographs you are still not in a position to complete a photographic assignment to the satisfaction of a customer. The transition between all the individual training routes and becoming a professional photographer is fluid. Practically every photographic assistant have completed an internship or professional training in photography and many students have completed an internship, often during their time at university. A number of architecture students take architectural photography courses during their studies and discover that their discipline involves more than just the planning of buildings.

Whichever route you take to becoming a photographer, technology and equipment, software and the picture market are developing fast and the tempo is increasing so photographers, whatever their background, must continue their professional development independently. And whatever path taken by the young photographer, patience is the single most important requirement, patience with others, and patience with oneself above all. Experience has shown that it takes years before the photographer is fully aware of his or her tastes and strengths and before he or she has developed an individual style.

Photographic skills, and this applies equally to interns, apprentices, assistants, students and independent students, can only develop and flourish with good equipment. This is usually provided initially by an employer, an instructor or an educational establishment. Once again, independent students have the hardest job. They are dependent on themselves alone and have nobody to point out errors and with a few exceptions, nor do they have access to a studio or a complete professional outfit worth tens of thousands of euros.

(10.2) — TAX AND INSURANCE

Trade photographers in Germany are obliged to register in the trades register and to pay subscriptions to the German chamber of commerce. For entrants to the profession it is financially more beneficial to apply to the tax authority for accreditation as a freelance architectural photographer. Anyone with accreditation does not have to pay business taxes. You are also exempt from the book-keeping and accounting obligation. In addition, German freelance photographers can obtain insurance from the Künstlersozialkasse (www.kuenstlersozialkasse.de) – the artists' social security fund. This means they pay only around half the sickness, healthcare and pension insurance contributions. The other half of the contributions is financed by a federal committee and by charges paid by companies using artistic and mass communication media services.

In Germany trade photographers and freelancers must obtain accident insurance cover from the professional association EnergieTextil Elektro Medienerzeugnisse (www.bgetem.de). If you work less than 100 days a year, however, you can exempt yourself from this obligation but you then need private accident insurance. Professional liability and professional indemnity insurance are important for any photographer. It may also be worthwhile ensuring your equipment.

Trade photographers and freelancers need to submit a tax return to the appropriate tax office each year. They are also obliged to show VAT on every invoice and to pay this to the tax office. Anyone employing an assistant or office staff needs to pay wage tax and contributions for healthcare, pension and unemployment insurance. Employers are also obliged to continue to pay wages during sickness and maternity leave. It is wise to set aside a contingency fund as soon as possible to cover for this. Before starting out as a full- or part-time photographer you should obtain as much information as you can from a tax lawyer or accountant.

(10.3) — MARKETING

Financial success, irrespective of the quality of your photographs, generally depends on how you attract potential customers and publicise your images, how you communicate with them and how you maintain communication. You should devise a self-marketing strategy including a timetable and financial budget which, particularly in the early years, should be quite generous. You are recommended to examine the success of your marketing efforts critically and honestly at regular intervals and to change your strategy if necessary.

Amongst the most important clients for architectural photographs are the publishers of specialist journals (see appendix). These are also important publications for any architect wishing to make his or her name in the business. The majority of the readership of these publications are architects, architecture students and promoters. But even these publications have been seeking to acquire photographs as cheaply as possible in recent years. Rather than buying photographs from photographers, they are trying to obtain free copyright from architects whose projects they are featuring. And recently architects have been expecting that the photographs that they have so far used only for brochures and homepages can be used by the press at no extra cost.

Other customers include exhibition stand producers wanting to furnish their stands with photographs of products, company buildings, production equipment and employees. Advertising agencies producing brochures and catalogues as well as book and press publishers are amongst the most important customers of architectural photographers. Since they have been under extreme cost pressure in recent years, they are also making increasing use of microstock agencies. For this they are willing to make greater compromises in terms of choice of image and picture quality for the sake of cutting extra costs.

For long-term success as a photographer you need to ensure that you are not undermining your own market and prices, for example by charging different prices to different customers. Since architects and other customers talk to one another, this is bound to come out sooner or later. Newcomers often make the error of working on the cheap in order to win contracts and access the market. Experience has shown, however, that customers will not be willing to pay a higher price for the same work at a later date. From the outset, therefore, you need to cover your costs and convince your customers that good work is worth paying for.

But how do you find your customers? You can research addresses of architects and building firms on the Internet and you can find them in the Yellow Pages and reference works, for example the Bund der Deutschen Architekten (www.bda-bund.de) and the architect chambers of the various German states.

At the end of the day, though, there is no substitute for knocking on doors. You need to get your name out and about and advertise. This includes a good website, business cards, exhibitions and participation in photographic competitions. You also need to contact your core customers regularly. Hardly any architectural photographer can afford to sit in the studio waiting for customers. Unlike portrait photography, the subject matter of architectural photography will not fit into a studio. You therefore need to be on the move with your equipment in the major cities wherever building projects are under way. You need to frequent the sites of the major firms and architectural bureaus.

Tried and tested tools and aids

There is a series of tried and tested tools and aids for the self-marketing of architectural photography. You need to choose which of them will give you the best results:

→ A business card should be your basic tool.

→ Every architectural photographer should put together a portfolio of his or her best photographs – freelance and contract work. The portfolio should be representative and high-quality but not over-large.

→ Having your own website gives interested parties the opportunity to find out about your actual work without making any commitment. Along with a short CV with an attractive portrait photo and contact details it should showcase a selection of successful examples of work. You should also include a list of exhibitions where your pictures can be seen, a list of references and a list of publications in the print media.

→ Participation in photographic competitions run by photographic journals is a good opportunity to test yourself as a photographer, to attract attention and to make contacts.

→ An essential part of your timetable is regular participation in exhibitions, photo festivals and art fairs.

To maintain contacts a lot of photographers invite their customers and friends and the regional press regularly to exhibitions in their own studios. An attractive invitation is a good reminder of who you are, even if not every invitee attends the exhibition.

→ To maintain contacts and keep abreast of new trends you should attend national and regional trade fairs, trade shows and open days for buildings and interiors, for example, Domotex (www.domotex.de) in Hanover, Deubau (www.deubau-essen.de) in Essen and Domicil (www.reichert-messen.de/Domicil.htm) in Frankfurt.

→ A flyer can bridge the gap between the business card and the portfolio and is ideal for distributing at trade fairs and exhibitions. Along with a short CV and a portrait photo it should display a series of sample photographs which will give interested parties an idea of your photographic style.

→ Classified ads in the trade press and in the daily and weekly regional press are a good, but not cheap, way of attracting attention. You should design them to attract the attention of the reader to you and they should include your website address. There are also possibilities for advertising on the Internet, for example Klicktel (www.klicktel.de), Gelbe Seiten (www.gelbeseiten.de), architekten24 (http://www.architekten24.de) and germanarchitects (www.german-architects.com).

→ Another important marketing tool is the press release. You should also always invite the regional press to your own exhibitions. When exhibiting, always issue a press release containing key information about the exhibition and at least one representative photograph which will be included in the exhibition. At the opening itself you should always provide a short biography with information about the focal points of your work and about the actual exhibition.

→ The most worthwhile method of getting contracts is and remains personal contact with potential customers by telephone, letter or email. Before each call you should find out as much about your contact as possible.

Rules of thumb for success

There is a handful of rules for marketing which it pays to take heed of:

→ Make your advertising fit your target group! Be clear about who your potential customers are. Only when you know your target customers and their needs and preferences can you produce the right advertising in the right advertising medium. The most important customers for architectural photographers are architects, construction firms, estate agents, construction materials manufacturers and retailers. Wholesalers and retailers, purchasing organisations and trade associations also always need interior architecture photographs for brochures and catalogues. The same applies to manufacturers and vendors of lighting for public roads, spaces and buildings and for the private domain.

→ Get to know your competitors! Analyse not just the photographs of established colleagues but also exactly how they sell themselves. Who makes their business cards, their flyers, their website? Where do they advertise? Where do they exhibit pictures? With which galleries and agencies do they work? Who are their clients?

→ Present yourself via a professional corporate image. Visual image plays a major role in architecture as in architectural photography. You should take this into account particularly in the development of your corporate image. Amateurish business cards or a cheap homepage will put off potential customers before you have even made contact. Your whole public image – business cards, letterhead, offers and invoices, flyers, brochures, posters and handouts – should be in the same style and should feature the same colours and design elements. The same applies to your homepage.

→ Create your own customer database! Include names and addresses of your customers plus information about their aims and preferences and about their building projects including completion dates. Also note when and where you have made contact with the customer and what agreements you have made. If you often work with larger companies you should include names, email addresses and mobile phone numbers of key contacts.

→ Find out regularly about impending and completed building projects whatever the scale. The architectural press is an ideal source of information as are relevant forums on the Internet.

→ Build up a network and keep it up to date. Most important are architects, building companies and other possible customers plus the building trade, exhibitors at trade fairs and exhibitions and specialist journalists from the area of building, interiors and architecture. In Germany you are also recommended to develop contacts in the press and publicity departments of the national architectural chambers and the state architectural chambers. Get included in their press distribution lists.

(10.4) —— QUOTATIONS, CALCULATIONS, OFFERS AND ORDERS

Before you set up your tripod and camera in front of a building and release the shutter you need to carry out a whole series of preparations. Almost every photographic order starts with a letter, usually open-ended, and the request from a customer to submit a tender. If you want to work long-term as a professional photographer you absolutely must have a basic commercial grounding. Two manuals *Basiswissen* (Basic knowledge) and *Verträge* (Contracts) available from the German photographers association Bundes der Freien Fotodesigner (BFF) are valuable aids.

It is standard practice in the business to calculate prices based on daily rates or unit costs. It makes sense in that case to use the recommended fees of the BFF or the Mittelstandsgemeinschaft Foto-Marketing (MFM) of the German press photography agency association Bundesverbands (BVPA) der Pressebildagenturen.

These provide not only suggested fees but also suggested periods of use, forms of use and methods of use. The MFM also suggests discounts and supplements, for example for poster formats and exclusive rights. In order to calculate a price it must be possible to calculate the actual costs. You need to take into account the following operational, preparation and administration costs:

Preparatory costs:

→ Rents
→ Personal
→ Electricity, water and heating
→ Equipment leasing

Operating costs:

→ Vehicle maintenance
→ Membership of professional associations
→ Servicing
→ Cleaning
→ Advertising
→ Insurance
→ Travel expenses
→ Repairs and maintenance
→ Postage and packing

Administration costs:

→ Professional development
→ Books and journals
→ Stationary
→ Telecommunication

Before submitting an offer to a potential customer you need to be clear about the exact scope of the order. Before agreeing a contract you also need to discuss whether the client wishes to purchase the images or the rights of use. In the first case, for instance, the photographer would supply finished framed prints for the decoration of a foyer, in the second, image data for websites. Finally you need to agree a date by when the contract is to be completed.

Architects and other customers often have specific expectations of the number and type of pictures they want to commission. It is also helpful to ask the client or architect what aims informed the building planning and the lighting concept. You should also ask what image statement and views the client wants. Just as often, however, a client will give the photographer free rein. In either case you need to find out even before submitting an offer the type, location, aspect and address of the property. It is always helpful if the client gives you a building specification and plans of the property. Ideally, you will visit the building to be photographed together with the client. This is not always possible, however. If your bid is accepted you should have this confirmed in writing along with the precise scope of the order.

→ The homepage of the Hamburg picture agency Artur Images which specialises in architecture.

(10.5) —— WORKING WITH PICTURE AGENCIES

An architectural photographer wanting to make a living from this work needs direct customers above all. Photographers normally do not sell all picture rights to their direct customers. Instead they sell rights of use for specific purposes and defined periods. You can then sell the same photographs to other customers. The two customers should not of course be in direct competition with one another.

Searching for buyers for existing pictures is the job of the picture agencies. Making a profit is primarily down to the multiple use of your photographs with the help of a picture agency. The largest agents are Corbis and Getty-Images in the USA and Mauritius-Images in Germany. Artur Images located in Hamburg is of particular interest. It began as a photographic association and specialises entirely in architectural photography. It represents about 90 architectural photographers.

The agencies charge their customers standard market rates depending on whether a picture is published in a book, a newspaper or a magazine. The fee depends on the medium, the number of editions, size of reproduction, duration of use, distribution and placement. This means that a considerably higher fee is obtained for a title picture than for a small picture on the back page. The most important guide to setting fees is the fee recommendations of the Mittelstandsgemeinschaft Foto-Marketing (MFM) in the Bundesverband der Pressebildagenturen (www.bvpa.org) in which fee rates are reset each year.

The fee income is divided between the agent and the photographer. The agencies normally receive 50 to 70 per cent of the sale income. The more photographs you place with an agency, the more subjects they can offer and sell and the more you can earn from agency work. As a photographer you need to bear in mind that agencies are in a position to reach customers which you could never reach yourself. However, buyers of pictures from agencies do know who took the photograph and, with a little luck, the buyer will come directly to you. You will then have won yourself a direct customer. You cannot normally sell pictures which you have placed with an agency elsewhere during the contract period. This rule applies of course only for photographs which are distributing via the agency. Photographs which you have not placed with the agency can be sold as normal.

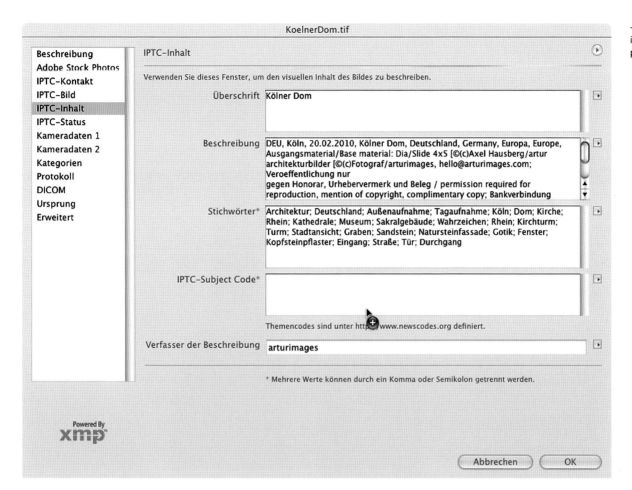

→ Careful tagging is important for photo-marketing.

If you want to work with a picture agency, you should consider first of all which agency your pictures will suit best. You need to approach this agency first with picture samples and a description of your key points. Agencies constantly need new and current picture material but the photographs must comply with defined quality standards. As an agency photographer you can get a taste of what is in demand in the marketplace. There is a constant demand for instance for photographs of current newbuild projects by famous architects and of buildings bearing logos of companies which are currently in the media. It is also worthwhile particularly for a beginner to ask an agency by telephone or by e-mail what properties are in demand at the moment and whether such images should feature people or not. Some agencies send subject lists to their photographers on a regular basis.

It is often a good idea to offer pictures which are somehow out of the ordinary, for instance with unusual image ideas or original perspectives. Wide-ranging images are also better than narrow perspectives as their scope of use is correspondingly wider. Unlike in other areas, traditional representations are still desirable in architectural photography.

You should therefore avoid deliberate alienation. You should rather offer the customer the opportunity to make their own alterations to the image in terms of colour and graphics, to incorporate them into montages or to crop the image. The photographer needs to clarify to the agency at the contract stage that the image can be altered. To avoid infringement claims, you should provide the agency with written assurance that the agency has all rights to the images placed for marketing.

Agency business is relatively time-consuming for a photographer. You need to digitise and tag each image. Good tagging is important for marketing. The better a photograph is tagged, the greater the probability that it will be found and the better it will sell in preference to similar pictures.

A view of Cologne Cathedral, for example, should be tagged with the following keywords: Germany, Cologne, church, cathedral, gothic, external view, daytime photograph, sandstone, cultural building, museum, public, sacred building, trademark, river, Rhine, water, church spire, tower, city view.

→ An unusual view of Cologne Cathedral

→ The homepage of the microstock agency fotolia

Microstock agencies and photographs in the public domain

Since the start of the 21st century, traditional picture agencies have been competing with so-called microstock agencies. Microstock agencies are picture agencies that offer photographs via the Internet at very reasonable rates. They differ from conventional agencies as follows:

→ They deal with photographers and with customers entirely via Internet portals.

→ They work with a broader range of photography.

→ They work with amateur photographers.

→ There is no individual personal consultation.

→ They offer low prices.

There are around 50 platforms including fotolia (de.fotolia.com), shutterstock images (www.shutterstock.com), iStockphoto (www.istockphoto.com), dreamstime (de.dreamstime.com), stockxpert (de.stockxpert.com), Photocase (www.photocase.com/de), 123RF.com (de.123rf.com) and panthermedia (www.panthermedia.net).

Microstock agencies have become possible ever since adequate digital cameras have been available for a few hundred euros and because nowadays many people have cost-effective access to broadband networks. The trend meets the growing emphasis of many photograph customers on price first and foremost. If the price is right, customers are prepared to compromise on picture quality. Microstock agencies can provide images for a few pence. The service offered to customers and photographers, however, is drastically less than with traditional agencies. Contact with customers as well as photographers is limited to the agency's Internet platform.

Anyone placing images with microstock agencies, provided the quality is right, will enjoy the steady trickle of pocket money. However, the fees are generally insufficient to live on and as customers get more and more used to the prices of microstock agencies, professional photographers are experiencing ever greater problems gaining sufficient income from their images. This is actually putting the whole profession at risk. Even the traditional picture agencies are increasingly threatened. The only chance for professional photographers is to offer unusual subject matter and views. The more photographs there are of a subject, the fewer the chances for the individual

→ The fotocommunity homepage

→ Wikimedia Commons is a sister project to Wikipedia.

photographer that his or her photograph of that subject will be bought. Opportunities therefore lie at the limits of the microstock agencies. These limits are frequently reached when a customer requires a photograph of a specific building, has specific requirements for the image or if the picture is required for a specific purpose. Architects therefore are still amongst the most loyal customers. If they need a photograph showing a building immediately after completion they will almost always have to appoint a professional photographer. Even then, however, prices are falling, partly because architects are not unaware of the marketplace.

From a financial perspective, microstock agencies are of little interest to professional photographers. On the other hand, they provide an almost inexhaustible fund of material to look at. You can find examples of nearly every pitfall for the photographer and you will also find plenty of very good photographs and a wealth of inspiration for choice of subject matter and execution. The community functions integrated into, for example, Fotocommunity (www.fotocommunity.de) allow you to exchange information with other photographers about subject matter, execution and equipment or even to arrange photo safaris. They also allow you to upload your own photographs for discussion.

Along with microstock, the Internet also has numerous other photographic sources which can be used free of charge, even commercially, because they are either copyrighted images provided under a free licence or because they have become public domain material due of the expiry of legal copyrights. Wikimedia Commons (http://commons.wikimedia.org) is one example. A sister project of Wikipedia, it is a universal collection of public domain photographs and other media files. 12 million files had been uploaded to this database as of January 2012. In Germany there is also an increasing number of city and regional Wikis whose photographs are generally provided under a free licence.

The photo portal Pixelio (www.pixelio.de) for example contained more than 420,000 pictures in 227 categories in January 2012. Users have to register with the site and log in before uploading or downloading photos. There is no need to register however to search within the hierarchical structure. Pixelio images are also free to use. Users are simply obliged to cite Pixelio as the source for the photos. Administrators appraise the images which are uploaded by users to the Pixelio server and release them provided they comply with the minimum requirements for quality and size. An active community of users has grown up around Pixelio, evaluating and discussing the photos. Photographers who upload their images to these platforms are generally amateurs (as on Wikipedia) who offer their photographs for general use free of charge. Photographers who want and need to make a living from their work are not terribly happy about microstock agencies and databases providing photographs free of charge. These platforms upset the prevailing price structure and the traditional business models.

→ A photograph of the Frankfurt shopping and leisure centre MyZeil including people as secondary subjects.

(10.6) — PHOTOGRAPHIC RIGHT IN PRACTICE USING FIVE LEGAL CASES

Christoph Gößmann

Given that photographic rights is a very complex amalgam of, principally, copyright, personal right and right of ownership, five popular legal cases from the practice of architectural photography will be cited to give some idea of the things that an architectural photographer needs to bear in mind.

Copyright

The right of the originator, that means the person who has created a work (architect, painter, photographer, author, etc.), must be respected. This right remains with the originator and can be passed on to heirs for 70 years in the event of his or her death. The scope of this protection is set out under the Copyright Act (Urheberrechtsgesetz – UrhG). One aspect of this protection is the originator's exclusive right of exploitation, according to which the originator must give their consent before their work is reproduced, distributed or exhibited.

If third parties are to be allowed to use works, the originator has the option to assign rights of use. This is done through licences that are grouped into exclusive and non-exclusive (so-called simple) licences. In addition, the geographical, temporal and content-related use can be defined more precisely. With the award of licences, a distinction is commonly made between the editorial and the commercial use of works.

1. Editorial: use within a reporting context (in an article, for example).

2. Commercial: use for the purpose of realising profits (advertisements, company website, for instance).

The same legal text (UrhG), however, also sets out copyright limitations (§§ 44a to 63a UrhG), where by far the most important copyright limitation as far as architectural photography is concerned is the freedom of panorama (§ 59 UrhG):

If a work is permanently located on public highways, streets or squares, a photograph of this work created without using any aids may be reproduced, distributed and communicated to the public. In the case of buildings, this rule applies only to the exterior.

Further limitations occasionally allow reporting on current events such as exhibition openings (to an extent appropriate for the purpose) and, in so doing, the depiction of copyright-protected works (§ 50 UrhG), the making of reproductions of works for private use (§ 59 UrhG) and the quoting of works (§ 51 UrhG). Note here that it is not only text that may be quoted but also, of course, pictorial citations. Acknowledgement to the source is obligatory with every reproduction (§ 63 UrhG).

One glance at the Copyright Act quickly puts right a number of misconceptions. For example, it is often claimed that with six people or more a group rule comes into play that allows the production and publication of photographs without permission. This rule does not exist. The decisive element in such a situation is whether an identifiable person can be regarded as an insignificant feature (§ 57 UrhG). If the effect of the photograph is not altered by the absence of this person, this usually means that there is no infringement of any rights, such as the right to one's own image. These copyright limitations do not just apply to people; they can also be applied analogously to objects such as paintings or a piece of furniture with a protected design.

If the right of the originator is violated, he or she is entitled to forbearance, disclosure and compensation. Amounts payable are based upon usual licence payments and do not allow mark-ups for an infringement of rights. By way of a warning, the conclusion of a declaration of forbearance may be required, which, in the event of any violation, provides for a contractual penalty in excess of the usual licence payments.

Personal right

Copyright is not the only stumbling block in photographic rights. It is also essential to remember to respect privacy rights in this context. One such right is the right to one's own image as mentioned above (§ 22 of the Art Copyright Act (Kunsturhebergesetz – KunstUrhG). According to this right, photographs may only be published with the consent of the individually identifiable person in the picture. Alongside the limitation set out in § 57 UrhG (insignificant feature), there are further limitations. Contemporary public figures, such as politicians, enjoy only limited protection, just as people who take part in gatherings, processions or similar events (§ 23 KunstUrhG).

The publication of an architectural photograph with mention of the exact location of the property and the name of the owner may also constitute an infringement of privacy. If there are plans to publish a picture of a photographed person, consideration should be given to drawing up a modelling contract setting out the scope of use of the photograph and any royalties. If a (private) property is to appear in a publication with mention of the location and the name of the owner, a written agreement with the rightholder is also advisable.

Right of ownership
While there is no right to the image of one's own property as a counterpart to the right to one's own image, the right of ownership does also provide for certain protection zones. The owner can exclude others from having any impact on his property (§ 903 of the German Civil Code (Bürgerliches Gesetzbuch – BGB)) and has a right to forbearance in the event of any impairment to their property (§ 1004 BGB).

The freedom of panorama (§ 59 UrhG) constitutes a limitation of the right of ownership. In a non-public area in which the freedom of panorama does not apply, or if copyright-protected objects are part of the photograph, a contract should be drawn up with the rightholder. The rightholder may, for example, be the owner of an estate on which photographs are taken or a painter whose paintings are part of the composition.

FIVE LEGAL CASES

1. Frisian cottage
A textile trader used a photo in his brochures depicting the front of a cottage built in the 1740s on the island of Sylt as visible from the road. The owner regarded the unauthorised production and commercial use of the photograph as an infringement of his right of ownership and a considerable invasion of his privacy, and sued for forbearance, withdrawal of promotional material already distributed and payment of DM 10,000.
The defendant held the view that there were no legal grounds to justify the action. He further contested the claim that the plaintiff had been spoken to by friends and acquaintances about the use of the photograph and about an associated identification, according to the plaintiff, with the defendant's products. Under these conditions, the plaintiff deemed that there had been a definite invasion of his privacy.

The Federal Court of Justice of Germany (BGH) ruled that the unauthorised photographing of a third-party house and the commercial exploitation of such a photograph do not constitute an impact on the third-party property that would trigger a right to defence and payment if the photograph is taken from a publicly accessible location without entering the grounds of the house (BGH, 09.03.1989 – I ZR 54/87).

In contrast to other legal cases involving architectural photography, in this specific case there had been no need to enter private grounds to take the photograph. Application of the freedom of panorama covered both the production and the exploitation of the photograph and meant that there was no infringement of the right of ownership.

Personal rights violations were excluded because the court took the view that reproduction of the image could not give the impression described by the plaintiff that the latter identified with the defendant's products. Furthermore, the plaintiff was unable to provide any evidence that he had been spoken to by friends and acquaintances in connection with this.

Decisive rules: Freedom of panorama.

2. Wrapped Reichstag
Between 24 June and 7 July 1995, husband-and-wife artists Christo and Jeanne-Claude wrapped the Reichstag building in Berlin in reinforced foil with a solid substructure made of steel. This striking work of art was the subject of numerous photographs by third parties that were used, for example, for daily news reports.
Given that the wrap artists funded the project partly through the commercial exploitation of photographs of the work of art, they took action against a photo agency that sold postcards depicting the wrapped Reichstag building. In the couple's view, originator's rights were violated by this unauthorised, commercial exploitation.
The photo agency referred in its defence to the freedom of panorama (§ 59 UrhG). However, the plaintiffs argued that the freedom of panorama should not apply in this case since the work was not permanently located on public highways, streets or squares.

The court agreed with the plaintiffs' argument and ruled in their favour. The erection was always intended to be for a limited time that was shorter than the natural lifespan of the work. It was also irrelevant whether the work would continue to exist after its removal. Since the work did not satisfy the criterion of "permanent", the freedom of panorama could not be applied. (BGH, 24.01.2002 – I ZR 102/99).

The robust material (fireproof polypropylene fabric) justifies the discrepancy between lifespan and time of public erection. However, for works that are in one place for their entire lifespan, even if this is only a few seconds, the freedom of panorama does apply. But reporting on current events (§ 50 UrhG) is possible without any problem even in the original situation. The same is true, for example, for exhibition openings even if the works enjoy copyright protection.

Decisive: Copyrights of the artists, criterion "permanent" in freedom of panorama.

3. Hundertwasser-Krawina House
Together with architects Josef Krawina and, later, Peter Pelikan, painter Friedensreich Hundertwasser drew up plans for an apartment complex for the

municipality of Vienna. German retailer the Metro Group sold the framed print of a photograph of this building completed in 1985 that was taken from a private residence opposite.

Hundertwasser's heirs saw the resulting elevated and non-public perspective as a reason to take legal action against the sale in Germany. They sued for forbearance, disclosure and compensation.

Metro relied in its defence on the freedom of panorama (§ 59 UrhG).

The Higher Regional Court (OLG) in Munich upheld the right to forbearance of Hundertwasser's heirs on the grounds that the right to reproduce a copyright-protected building using a photograph only covers photographs taken from a location generally accessible to the public.
The claim for disclosure and compensation was rejected (OLG Munich, 16.06.2005 – 6 U 5629/99).

The decision to reject the claim for disclosure and compensation is not really of interest to architectural photographers. The reasons for this had to do with licensing law. What is more interesting is the fact that even though the photograph was lawfully taken and sold in Austria on the basis of Austria's more liberal counterpart to Germany's freedom of panorama (§ 54 of the Austrian Copyright Act), the legal position in Germany is very different. The approach follows the country of protection principle, which states that the law of the state for whose territory (copyright) protection is claimed must always be applied.

With the entry into force of Directive 2001/29/EC, copyright was meant to have been harmonised throughout Europe by 2002. Despite these efforts, as this case shows, there is no congruence between court decisions. This should be a first indication that outside Germany, particularly in countries outside Europe, there are completely different rules on the freedom of panorama, if it even exists at all.

Decisive: Copyright of the artist, criterion "public" in freedom of panorama

4. Prussian Palaces and Gardens Foundation

The Prussian Palaces and Gardens Foundation (SPSG) curates a number of cultural heritage sites including the baroque Sanssouci Palace. This is surrounded by a spacious garden, making it difficult to see from outside. For photographs taken for commercial purposes of the foundation's own listed buildings and monuments, their furnishings and the gardens, the foundation reserves the right to impose on the photographer the obligation to obtain a written declaration of consent.

In this specific case, the SPSG sued a company giving photographers the chance to offer their pictures to a wider market via the Internet. The defendant only provides the technical platform of a virtual marketplace. However, what is important to consider here is not the responsibility of the operator of the picture platform, but rather the findings made during the proceedings that constituted extensive rights for the SPSG. The case was heard by the Potsdam Regional Court, then by the Brandenburg Higher Regional Court and finally by the Federal Court of Justice of Germany.

Overturning the previous verdict of Brandenburg Higher Regional Court, which emphasised that the foundation's right of ownership was confined to protection of the material substance, the Federal Court of Justice of Germany derived from the right of ownership the exclusive right of the SPSG to produce and exploit photographs taken from its grounds (BGH, 17.12.2010 – V ZR 45/10; V ZR 46/10; V ZR 44/10).

It should be noted that photographs of the foundation's cultural heritage sites taken in compliance with the freedom of panorama (that means from outside the grounds) are not, of course, affected by the SPSG's exclusive right to produce and exploit photographs.

Incidentally, throughout the entire process, it was never clarified unequivocally whether the SPSG really is the owner of the cultural heritage sites entrusted to its care. However, to be on the safe side, it should be assumed that this is so.

One way around the SPSG's exclusive right to produce and exploit photographs is to take aerial photographs, for which authorisation has not been required since 1990. The production of such images should not pose any problems since the expiry of copyrights 70 years after the death of the originator (§ 64 UrhG) means that there are no longer any claims on the part of the architects or their heirs and also because the distance from the subject and its public nature mean that personal rights are not usually violated.

If one wanted to generalise this case, § 109 of the German Penal Code (Strafgesetzbuch – StGB) would become relevant. This states that taking photographs of military installations, etc. is not permitted if the photographer knows that doing so will jeopardise the security of the Federal Republic of Germany or the effectiveness of the armed forces.

Decisive: Rights of ownership, end of the usual protection period (Europe-wide: 70 years after the death of the originator).

5. Tegel Palace

The Berlin district of Tegel is home to the privately owned Tegel Palace set in its own parkland. This is inhabited by the owners, who allow the public to enter the estate on payment of a fee. Once inside, people can buy picture postcards sold by the owner.

A photographer commissioned by a picture publishing company produced a photograph of the palace, which was then sold by the company in the form of postcards.

The owner, who permits the production of photographs for private use, subsequently sued for forbearance of the publication and sale of the photograph concerned. He deemed that this behaviour constituted an infringement of his right of ownership and, given the competition with the sale of picture postcards, unfair competition and a violation of his right to carry on a business.

The defence invoked the expiry of the copyright protection period and the fact that, when asked, employees of the owner said, without reservation, that photographs could be produced. It also argued that in this case there was a social commitment attached to ownership (ownership-associated obligation of use in the public interest).

<u>In contrast to a previous verdict in these proceedings, which derived a right to forbearance not from the right of ownership but from the apparently unethical exploitation of the competition, the Federal Court of Justice of Germany ruled in favour of a right to forbearance resulting from the right of ownership. The Federal Court of Justice of Germany further recognised the owner's prerogative to claim for himself the commercial benefit that can be derived from his property (which is only accessible with his consent). It said that he was free, in principle, to refuse entry or to allow entry only on the condition that photographs were not taken there. He alone could reserve the right to do so. A social commitment attached to ownership was not recognised in this case (BGH, 20.09.1974 – I ZR 99/73).</u>

What is interesting about this case is not necessarily how the plaintiff's right to forbearance was enforced but the fact that in this case permission to take photographs without an explicit limitation to photographs for private purposes does not entail permission for commercial exploitation. The owner is free, in principle, to refuse entry or to allow entry only on the condition that photographs are not taken there.

<u>Decisive: Right of ownership (§§ 903, 1004 BGB)</u>

Chapter 11
Appendix

272 Glossary
278 Literature
280 Directory of links
284 Index

(11.1) —— GLOSSARY

Aberration, chromatic
Chromatic aberration (Greek: *chroma* = colour; Latin: *aberrare* = to deviate) refers to an image defect of optical lenses resulting from the fact that lenses have a different refractive index for different wavelengths of light (the dispersion of the lens). This phenomenon is particularly evident along boundaries that separate dark and light parts of the image and is manifested in green and magenta fringes.

Aliasing
The rectangular shape and the grid arrangement of sensor cells in a digital back can lead to diagonal lines appearing to be stepped. This phenomenon is called the stepping effect or aliasing.

Analogue-to-digital convertor
Analogue-to-digital convertors transform the light which encounters an optical sensor into digital electronic signals which can then be processed or saved (see also: Digital back).

Angle mirror
An angle mirror or mirror box is a view camera module designed to reverse the upside-down image of a subject on the focusing screen at the camera. Angle mirrors are attached behind the focusing screen.

Angle of view
The angle of view is the angle detected by a lens and is a measurement of the size of the subject of the photograph when projected onto the picture plane. This measurement depends on the focal length of the lens, on the size of the sensor or film and on the lens construction.

Anti-Scheimpflug
The anti-Scheimpflug rule makes it possible to soften unimportant or invasive parts of the image so that they disappear leaving only a very small subject area in focus (see also Scheimpflug principle).

Axis, optical
The optical axis in photography is the axis running through the centre of the camera's lens system.

Black point
The black point when taking a photograph is the darkest area of a subject and, if scanning, is the darkest pixel of a picture (see also: White point).

Black value
Black value of a monitor is the darkest colour value which the monitor can display. For technical reasons many monitors are not able to display absolute black.

Blended light
We speak of blended light when lights with different colour values meet in the image subject. The most frequent case is daylight mixed with artificial light.

Calibration
Calibration refers to the interaction of equipment, software and working processes.

Centre filter
A centre filter is a neutral grey graduated filter which is lighter towards the outer edge in order to compensate for the loss of brightness towards the outside edge with extremely wide-angle view lenses with a particularly large image circle.

Centrefold
The centrefold is a picture error in which one half of an image is lighter than the other. It is caused by the sensor design. Software is available to correct this error.

Chromaticity diagram
A chromaticity diagram is a two-dimensional reproduction of the three-dimensional colour space.

Circular level
A circular level is a glass or plastic enclosure filled with a gas bubble which is used, like a spirit level, for horizontal and vertical alignment of the camera.

Colorimeter
Colorimeters are designed to measure colour intensities and colour temperatures of monitors and photographs and other reflective images. They are needed to calibrate monitors and printers (see also: Colour temperature meter).

Colour cast
Colour cast refers to patches of colour variation which can occur during shift and tilt adjustments with digital backs. These colour variations, usually magenta or green, radiate outwards. The colour cast is individual to each lens but like a fingerprint it is constant within each lens. Manufacturers of digital backs provide software which is able to compensate for this error for any lens from the image file.

Colour depth
Colour depth, also known as bit planes or pixel depth, defines how many colour tones each pixel of an image or a photograph can have.

Colour fringe
The colour fringe is a picture error which can occur when photographing with digital backs. It manifests as a narrow strip of colour along sharp edges

with high contrast. The cause of this problem is the lens. Particular culprits are wide-angle retrofocus lenses which are configured for analogue photography. Lenses configured for digital photography do not suffer from this problem.

Colour interpolation
In digital photography every pixel is composed of different brightness values of the three basic colours, red green and blue. Optimally, therefore, each sensor, cell would reflect the brightness values of all three colours. For technical reasons, however, sensor cells can only perceive one colour. Therefore the cells of the image sensors are arranged in groups of four and a miniature colour filter is placed in front of each individual cell. In general, two of each of the four-cell groups is green sensitive. One cell is blue sensitive and the fourth cell is red sensitive. To obtain a full RGB value for every pixel, however, the camera software calculates the missing colour values for each sensor cell from the colour values of its three neighbouring cells. This process is called colour interpolation.

Colour space
Colours are not represented absolutely faithfully by photographic systems, that means by image sensors and analogue-to-digital converters. In reality there are infinite colours. Photographic systems can only replicate a limited number, however. When developing colour models the aim is to make the available colours as close as possible to real-life colours. The three-dimensional representation of this kind of colour model is called the colour space. The best known colour spaces are the RGB (for Red Green and Blue) and the CMYK (Cyan Magenta and Yellow-Key).

Colour temperature
The colour temperature is a measurement used to characterise the colour of light emitted by a light source. It is usually given in the unit Kelvin (K). Normal sunlight has a colour temperature of 5500 Kelvin (KE), candlelight has a colour temperature of 1500 Kelvin (see also: Twilight/dawn, Colour temperature meter).

Colour temperature meter
Modern colour temperature meters not only give the colour temperature of light; they also tell you what colour a lens filter needs to achieve a neutral colour temperature of 5500 Kelvin (see also Colorimeter).

Compendium
A compendium is an adjustable lens hood module which can be attached to a view camera in front of the lens.

Composing
Composing or collage in photography refers to photographs which are composed from parts of several other photographs or picture elements. There is a seamless transition between this and computer generated imaging.

Computer-generated imaging
Computer-generated imaging refers to the artificial production of images which look like photographs.

Copyright
Copyright is the right of the creator, for instance the poet, the painter, the photographer or the architect, to his or her own work.

Depth of field
When the lens and the picture plane of a camera are parallel to one another there is an area between two planes which are parallel to the lens and the picture plane which is in focus. The depth of this area is called the depth of field.

Digital back
A digital back or chip back is a digital photography system comprising an image sensor, an analogue-to-digital converter and a storage medium and can normally be adapted to different camera systems.

Distortion
Distortion describes a lens error in which straight lines are shown as bowed. Barrel distortion describes lines which are outwardly bowed, while inward bowing is described as pincushion distortion.

dpi
The resolution of optical equipment is frequently given in dpi (dots per inch), that means in pixels per 2.54 centimetres (see: Resolution, Resolving power).

Dual Scheimpflug
It is sometimes necessary for a subject plane which is both diagonally and horizontally tilted to the camera to be in focus. To overcome such difficulties, modern view cameras permit a double sharpness plane adjustment according to the general Scheimpflug rule.

Focussing screen
The focussing screen is the projection surface made of transparent material which is used in single lens reflex and view cameras to monitor the image composition and frame and to focus the lens.

Fresnel lens
Fresnel lenses are used to brighten the focusing screen. The name of this composite lens comes from

Augustin Jean Fresnel, who invented it in 1822. The Fresnel lens design principle comes from the lighthouse and was used to reduce weight and volume.

Gamma value
Gamma value tells you what brightness value to use to correct a 50 per cent grey of a monitor in order that the viewer will perceive a grey with exactly half that brightness. Because the human eye distinguishes between light colours better than dark ones, a 50 per cent grey therefore is not perceived as a grey of exactly half the brightness. The optimum value for PC systems is 2.2 and for Mac computers it is 1.8.

Grey balance
Colour-neutral grey values in colour printing are not produced with black and white pixels but, like all the other colours, with a mix of cyan, magenta and yellow. If the grey balance of a print is incorrect, neutral grey values will have a colour cast.

Grey card
A grey card is made of plastic or paper and depicts a standardised grey value which reflects 18 per cent of the incidental light. Grey cards are used in photography to control brightness and colour values.

Greyscale wedge
A greyscale wedge is a strip of card or plastic with 19 different grey values from black to white. Greyscale wedges are used to calibrate contrast, brightness and colour of monitors, scanners and printers.

Helical focus mount
Unlike lenses of small-format cameras, view lenses do not have inbuilt focusing aids. To focus these lenses, you need a bellows or a helical focus mount. A helical focus mount is a tube which can be lengthened or shortened by means of a screw thread.

High-key photography
High-key photography is a type of photography dominated by soft pale light and minimal contrast (see also: Low-key photography).

Histogram
A histogram in digital photography refers to the visualisation of the statistical frequencies of the grey and colour values and the range of contrast and brightness of an image.

Image circle
Lenses always create circular images with different diameters depending on the design of the lens. These circles are called image circles. However, cameras always use rectangular segments of these image circles (see also: Angle of view).

IT-8
IT-8 refers to a standard for calibrating scanners, digital cameras, monitors and printers. It was developed to guarantee binding colour reproduction within process chains.

Large-format camera
Large-format cameras are cameras with image formats of 9 × 12 centimetres. View cameras are large-format cameras when they are modular in design and offer adjustment options (see also: View camera).

Lens flare
Lens flare is a lens-shaped circular or annular fringe of light on a photograph which is caused by flare reflections in the lens.

Lens hood
The lens hood is designed to prevent light coming from the side falling on the film or censor because this would otherwise be reflected on the lenses or in the lens barrel. These reflections lead to colour errors, reduce contrast and cause lens flare, lens-shaped circular or anular fringes of light. The picture quality as a whole is considerably reduced by these reflections, often rendering photographs unusable.

Light measurement
In photography light measurement refers to the way in which the brightness of the light falling on the subject is measured (see also: Object measurement).

Lines, converging
Converging lines result when a camera is tilted horizontally or vertically. The subject and/or the sensor or film planes cannot then be aligned in parallel. Therefore parallel subject lines will meet at a vanishing point within or outside the picture.

Live view
Live view or live preview refers to digital optical systems which allow you to monitor and adjust the picture segment and sharpness via a display. In this process the electronic image signal is transferred from the sensor to the display in real time.

Low-key photography
Low-key photography is a type of photography dominated by dark colours and high contrast (see also: High-key photography).

Manual spotlights
Manual spotlights focus the light through a lens whereby the light cone emitted by the spotlight can be redirected by flaps known as barn doors. Manual spotlights are used, for example, to light architectural models.

Microlens array
The microlens array is spoken of in photography when a microscopic lens array is placed in front of each cell in an image sensor. These lenses are used to realign diagonally-falling light to increase the light yield.

Microstock agency
A microstock agency offers photographs on particularly favourable terms. They differ from traditional picture agencies in that they receive and sell photographs entirely over the Internet and they also sell photographs from amateur photographers.

Moiré effect
The moiré effect is an interference pattern created, for example, when lines or grids are overlaid at an angle or when they have slightly different mesh sizes, for example if a striped or checked shirt is photographed with a digital back.

Motion blur
Motion blur is caused when a light from a flash, a torch or other light source moves within the photographic subject during a long exposure.

Normal focal length
A normal focal length is the focal length which corresponds to the diagonals of the photograph format. The regular focal length is not, as is often erroneously assumed, defined by the angle of vision of the eye.

Object measurement
Object measurement refers in photography to the type of exposure measurement used to measure the brightness of the light reflected from the subject. Since this is always based on an average brightness value, incorrect exposures are calculated for excessively bright or dark subjects (see also Light measurement).

Object plane
The object plane is the plane of the subject which you want to appear in focus on the photo. The sharply focused object plane is described as the plane of best sharpness.

Optical bench
An optical bench in photography is a monorail onto which the modules of a view camera are mounted.

Parallax errors
We speak of parallax error when the optical axes of the viewfinder and the lens are different. This error is particularly manifest in the close-up range of view cameras. In large-format cameras it is only a problem when stitching with the lens plane.

Photogrammetry
Photogrammetry is the zero-contact remote sensing and survey of buildings, site formations or other three-dimensional objects based on photography.

Picture plane
The picture plane is the sensor or film plane of a camera or of a similar optical system. Focusing the camera is generally designed to project a sharp image of the photographed subject onto this plane.

PostScript format
PostScript format has become the standard output format of image setters in graphic design and in the print industry. In this format 256 tonal values with respectively 256 greyscale levels are possible.

Rapid slide changer
A rapid slide changer is a view camera module which is used for multiple exposures and for quick and easy switching between the focusing screen and the photographic medium.

Refraction blurring
Refraction blurring is the loss of image sharpness resulting from the bending of light rays on the aperture ring of photographic lenses and other optical equipment. The smaller the aperture ring opening, the more obvious this generally unwanted effect.

Resolution
The resolution of a scanner is given in dots per inch (dpi), that means in pixels per 2.54 centimetres. This number is the measurement of the detail accuracy with which the scanner, but also the camera and other optical equipment, can scan a subject, a photograph, a positive or a negative (see also Resolving power).

Resolving power
Resolving power is the maximum resolution of an optical device. It is given in dots per inch (dpi), that means in pixels per 2.54 centimetres. The resolving power is an important variable for the characterisation of lenses, film material, digital sensors, scanners and other optical equipment (see also: Resolution).

Retrofocus lens
When photographing in the wide-angle range with view cameras you need to reduce the distance between the standards as far as possible. However, this reduces the mechanical adjustment possibilities. Retrofocus lenses have been designed to resolve this problem. Despite short focal lengths, they permit greater distances between the film and the lens plane.

Scan back
While chip backs record all pixels at once, scan backs read picture information in rows. The most important advantage of scan backs is that they offer considerably greater resolution and detail accuracy. Disadvantages are that they are not suitable for photographing moving subjects. Scan backs are predominantly used for reproductions and for photographing non-moving subjects in the studio.

Scheimpflug principle
The Scheimpflug principle was formulated in 1907 by the Austrian officer and cartographer Theodor Scheimpflug (1865–1911). It states that when the picture, lens and subject planes are parallel to one another or if they converge at the same point, the overall subject plane will be in focus (see also: Anti-Scheimpflug; Dual Scheimpflug).

Shift camera
A shift camera is a camera with a fixed lens. The shift option, unlike with a shift lens, is not integrated into the lens but into the camera housing.

Shifting
Shifting is the deliberate shifting of the picture with respect to the lens plane for the purposes of correcting perspective.

Standards
Standards are view camera modules. They hold lenses, focusing screens, digital backs, film cassette, bellows and connect them to the optical bench.

Stitching
Stitching or tiling is referred to when several photographs are taken of different sections within the picture circle of the lens and are subsequently stitched together on the computer to form an overall photograph during the digital image processing stage.

Swing
To swing an image is to deliberately rotate the image with respect to the lens plane. Like tilting it is used to adjust sharpness.

Telephoto lens
Telephoto lenses are lenses whose focal length is considerably longer than the camera extension due to a special lens construction. They were designed to reduce the problems of longer focal lengths with compact cameras (see also: Retrofocus lens).

Tilt
Tilt refers to the increasing of the depth of field by masking or by adjusting the camera according to the Scheimpflug rule (see also: Scheimpflug principle).

Tonal range
The tonal range of a picture refers to the number of shades between the brightest and darkest points. In digital processing up to 256 shades of any colour are standard (see also: Histogram).

Twilight/dawn
Twilight/dawn; respectively the time between the sun going down and the darkness of night and the time shortly before the sun comes up in the morning. During this period, the sky has a dark blue colour with a colour temperature of between 9,000 and 1,200 Kelvin (see also: Colour temperature).

Vanishing point
If you extend the parallel lines of a real building shown in perspective, these lines will converge at a single vanishing point (see also: Vanishing point perspective).

Vanishing point perspective
Buildings comprise perpendicular lines in three dimensions: height, width and depth. The camera perspective can be selected to create one, two or three vanishing points or more if you have reflections in the subject. A perspective with vanishing points is described as a vanishing point perspective.

View camera
The name refers to medium or large-format cameras which were designed for the two specialist areas of product photography and architectural photography. They are modular in design with individual modules being attached to an optical bench or mono rail. The most important modules are the bellows, the picture standard, the back and the front panel with the lens (see also: Large-format camera).

White balance
The white balance is used to adjust the camera to the colour temperature of the light prevailing when the photograph is being taken. The aim is authentic replication of the lighting mood on the photograph.

White point
The white point when taking a photograph is the lightest point of the subject and, when scanning, the lightest pixel of a picture (see also: Black point).

XY camera
XY cameras have neither bellows nor optical bench. In this camera type the picture standard can be adjusted horizontally (X-axis) and vertically (Y-axis). The distance between the picture and the lens standards is fixed. In the traditional view camera however both the picture and the lens standards can be adjusted horizontally and vertically.

(II.2) — BIBLIOGRAPHY

History of Architectural Photography

Benjamin, Walter: Kleine Geschichte der Photographie, in: Das Kunstwerk im Zeitalter seiner technischen Reproduzierbarkeit, Frankfurt/Main: 1966.

Eastman, George: The Kodak Primer, in: Coe, B.: Das erste Jahrhundert der Photographie, 1800–1900, Munich: 1979.

Eder, J. M.: Geschichte der Fotografie, Halle: 1923.

Feininger, Andreas: Andreas Feiningers große Fotolehre, Munich: 2001.

Feininger, Andreas: Die hohe Schule der Fotografie, Munich: 2005.

Frizot, Michel: Neue Geschichte der Fotografie, Cologne: 1998.

Gernsheim, Helmut: A Concise History of Photography, New York: 1986.

Tausk, Petr: Die Geschichte der Fotografie im 20. Jahrhundert, Cologne: 1986.

Turner, Peter: History of photography, Twickenham: 1987.

History and Theory of Architectural Photography

Adriani, Götz: In Szene gesetzt. Architektur in der Fotografie der Gegenwart, Ostfildern: 2002.

Architektur- und Städtefotos. Die Kodak Enzyklopädie der kreativen Fotografie, Amsterdam: 1985.

Bielefeld, Bert (Hg.): Basics Architekturfotografie, Basel: 2008.

Brüggemann, Jens/Daniel Kötz: Fotografie und Recht. Die wichtigsten Rechtsfälle für die Fotopraxis, Bonn: 2009.

Eibelshäuser, Eib: Fotografische Lichtgestaltung. Bessere Fotos durch gekonnte Lichtführung, Heidelberg: 2009.

Eisele, Reinhard: Architekturfotografie. Standpunkte, Techniken, Wirkungen, Augsburg: 1997.

Kopelow, Gerry: How to Photograph Buildings and Interiors, 2002.

Kopelow, Gerry: Architectural Photography: The Digital Way, 2007.

Kunert, Andreas: Farbmanagement in der Digitalfotografie, Bonn: 2004.

Lowe, Jim: Architectural Photography. Inside and Out, Lewes: 2006.

Maassen, Wolfgang: Verträge. Vertragsmuster, Formular, Musterverträge für Fotografen, Bildagenturen, Werbeagenturen, Repräsentanten, Stuttgart: 2006.

Mand, Katja: Das offene Bild. Auf der Suche nach dem "mehr" für die Architekturfotografie, Kassel: 2001.

Marchesi, Jost J.: Photokollegium. Ein Selbstlehrgang über die technischen Grundlagen der Photographie, Gilching: 2001.

Marchesi, Jost J.: Photokollegium, Gilching: 2007.

Rössing, Roger: Architekturfotografie, Leipzig: 1987.

Sachsse, Rolf: Photographie als Medium der Architekturinterpretation. Studien zur Geschichte der deutschen Architekturphotographie im 20. Jahrhundert, Munich: 1984.

Sachsse, Rolf: Architekturfotografie des 19. Jahrhunderts. Stationen der Fotografie, 6, Berlin: 1988.

Sachsse, Rolf: Bild und Bau. Zur Nutzung technischer Medien beim Entwerfen von Architektur, Wiesbaden: 1997.

Schulz, Adrian: Architekturfotografie – Technik, Aufnahme, Bildgestaltung und Nachbearbeitung, Heidelberg: 2008.

Shulman, Julius: Photographing Architecture and Interiors, Glendale: 2000.

Sigrist, Martin C./Stolt Matthias: Gestalten mit Licht. Lichtführung – Tageslichtaufnahmen – Blitztechnik, Munich: 2004.

Staiger, Uli: Foto-Composings, Bonn: 2007.

Tillmanns, Urs: Kreatives Großformat, volume 2: Architekturfotografie, Gilching: 1993.

Wick, Rainer K. (ed.): Das Neue Sehen. Von der Fotografie am Bauhaus zur Subjektiven Fotografie, Munich: 1991.

Monographs

Becher, Bernd und Hilla: Grundformen, Munich: 1999.

Belting, Hans: Thomas Struth. Museum Photographs, Munich: 1993.

Blossfeldt, Karl: Das fotografische Werk, Munich: 1981.

Dechau, Wilfried/Michel, Bettina (Hg.): Visionen in der Architektur. Europäischer Architekturfotografie-Preis 2001, Stuttgart: 2001.

Feininger, Andreas: Feininger's Chicago 1941, New York: 1980.

Lemoine, Bertrand: Gustave Eiffel, Paris: 1984.

Michel, Bettina (ed.): Architekturfotografen. Wer fotografiert Architektur in Deutschland, volume 1 and 2, Stuttgart: 1999 and 2001.

Rössing, Roger: Architekturfotografie, Leipzig: 1987.

(II.3) —— DIRECTORY OF LINKS

(II.3.1) —— MANUFACTURERS OF PHOTOGRAPHIC EQUIPMENT

View cameras
→ Arca-Swiss Snap-Studios – www.arca-shop.de
→ Alpa – www.alpa.ch
→ Sinar – www.sinar.ch
→ Cambo – www.cambo.com
→ Horseman – www.komamura.co.jp/e
→ Linhof – www.linhof.de
→ Plaubel – www.plaubel.com
→ Silvestri – www.silvestricamera.com
→ Seitz Phototechnik – german.roundshot.ch

Digital backs
→ Hasselblad – www.hasselblad.de
→ Phase One – www.phaseone.com
→ Sinar – www.sinar.ch/de/produkte/digitalrueckteile
→ Leaf – www.leaf-photography.com

View lenses
→ LINOS – www.rodenstock-photo.com

Tripods
→ Berlebach – www.berlebach.de
→ Bilora – www.bilora.de
→ Cullmann – www.cullmann-foto.de
→ FOBA – www.foba.ch
→ Giottos – www.giottos.de
→ Gitzo – www.gitzo.com
→ Manfrotto – www.manfrotto.com
→ Novoflex – www.novoflex.com
→ Sachtler – www.sachtler.com
→ Slik – www.slik.com
→ Velbon – www.velbon.co.uk

Film and photographic paper
→ Adox – www.adox.de
→ Bergger Photographic – www.bergger.com
→ Foma Bohemia – www.foma.cz
→ Fuji – www.fujifilm.de
→ Ilford – www.ilfordphoto.com
→ Kodak – www.kodak.com
→ Macodirect – macodirect.de

Filters
→ B & W/Schneider (Kreuznach) – www.schneiderkreuznach.com
→ Cokin – www.cokin.fr
→ Hama – www.hama.de
→ Heliopan – www.heliopan.de
→ Hoya – www.hoyafilter.com
→ LEE Foto-Filter – www.leefiltersusa.com
→ Rodenstock – www.rodenstock-photo.com

Exposure and colour temperature meters
→ Gossen – www.gossen-photo.de
→ Kenko – www.hapa-team.de
→ Minolta – www.konicaminolta.eu
→ Polaris – www.hensel.eu
→ Sekonic – www.sekonic.com

Flash systems
→ Balcar – www.balcar.com
→ Bläsing – blaesing.cfmx.de
→ Briese – www.briese-lichttechnik.de
→ Broncolor – www.bron.ch
→ Elinchrom – www.elinchrom.com
→ Hensel – www.hensel.eu
→ Horst Musch – www.musch-gmbh.de
→ Multiblitz – www.multiblitz.de
→ ProFoto – www.profoto.de
→ Richter – www.richterstudio.de

Accessories for flash equipment and lighting
→ California Sunbounce – www.sunbounce.com
→ Chimera – www.chimeralighting.com
→ Manfrotto – www.manfrotto.com
→ NorthLights – www.northlightproducts.com
→ Richter – www.richterstudio.de

HDR software
→ AGS Technik (FDRTools) – www.fdrtools.com
→ Franzis Verlag (Photomatix) – www.franzis.de
→ Idruna (Photogenics) – www.idruna.com
→ Lasersoft (SilverFast HDR) – www.silverfast.com
→ Qtpfsgui (Open Source) – qtpfsgui.sourceforge.net

Laboratory machinery, drying cabinets, film driers
→ Colenta – www.colenta.com
→ JOBO – www.jobo.com
→ Kindermann – www.kindermann.de

Laboratory chemicals
→ JOBO/Fuji – www.jobo.com
→ Kodak – www.kodak.com
→ Tetenal – www.tetenal.de

Scanners
→ Canon (CanoScan 8,800 F) – www.canon.de
→ Epson (Perfection V750 Pro, Expression 10,000 XL) – www.epson.de
→ Hasselblad (X1, X5, Imacon Flextight) – www.hasselblad.de
→ Nikon (Super Coolscan LS-9,000 ED) – www.nikon.de

Image processing and scanning software
→ Adobe (Photoshop) – www.adobe.com
→ Corel (PhotoImpact, Paint Shop Pro, Photo Paint) – www.corel.de
→ Gimp (Open Source) – www.gimp.org

→ LaserSoft (SilverFast) – www.silverfast.com
→ Microsoft (Foto Suite) – www.microsoft.com

Archiving programs
→ Adobe (Lightroom, Photoshop, Photoshop Elements, Album) – www.adobe.com
→ Acdsee (Foto-Manager) – de.acdsee.com
→ Apple (Aperture) – www.apple.com/de/aperture
→ Canto (mediadex) – www.canto.com
→ Hasselblad Phocus – www.hasselblad.com
→ Imation (OpdiTracker) – www.imation.com
→ IN MEDIA (Fotoarchiv Plus) – www.mediakg.de
→ Vallen (Jpegger) – www.vallen.de

Cutting equipment
→ C & H – www.framingsupplies.com
→ Dahle – www.dahle.de
→ Fletcher – www.fletcherviscom.com
→ Ideal – www.ideal.de
→ Kaiser – www.kaiser-fototechnik.de
→ Keencut – www.keencut.de
→ Logan – www.logangraphic.com
→ ProfiLine – www.biedermanngmbh.com
→ Rotatrim – www.rotatrim.co.uk
→ Valiani – www.valiani.com

Finishing accessories
→ Boesner – www.boesner.com
→ Canson – www.canson-infinity.com/de
→ Fotoimpex – www.fotoimpex.de
→ Gerstaecker – www.gerstaecker.de
→ Klug Conservation – www.klug-conservation.com
→ LEHA – www.leha.de
→ Monochrom – www.monochrom.com
→ Römerturm – www.roemerturm.de

Picture framing
→ Deha – www.deha-design.de
→ Halbe – www.halbe-rahmen.de
→ Max Aab – www.max-aab.de
→ Nielsen – www.nielsen-design.de
→ Roggenkamp – www.roggenkamp-bilderrahmen.de

Miscellaneous accessories
→ Arca-Swiss (cameras and tripod heads) – www.arca-shop.de
→ FOBA (tripods, tripod heads, studio accessories) – www.foba.ch
→ Gitzo (tripods and tripod heads) – www.gitzo.de
→ Hensel (tripods and tripod heads) – www.hensel.eu
→ Manfrotto (tripods and tripod heads) – www.manfrotto.de
→ Velbon (tripods and tripod heads) – www.velbon.co.uk
→ Zörk (camera- and shiftadapter) – www.zoerk.de

(II.3.2) —— SOURCES OF SUPPLY FOR PHOTO ACCESSORIES

→ Brakensiek – www.brakensiek.de
→ Calumet – www.calumetphoto.de
→ gfh-foto – www.gfh-foto.de
→ K.-D. Seynsche Fotolaborservice – www.fotolaborservice.de
→ Lotus View Camera – www.lotusviewcamera.at
→ Lumière – www.lumiere-shop.de
→ Martina Wehmeyer – www.bildservice-wehmeyer.de
→ Nordfoto – www.nordfoto.de
→ PhoBaTec – phobatec.com
→ Snap-Studios – www.arca-shop.de

(II.3.3) —— FESTIVALS AND TRADE FAIRS FOR PHOTOGRAPHY AND ART

→ Art Basel – www.artbasel.com
→ ART COLOGNE – www.artcologne.de
→ Darmstädter Tage der Fotografie – www.dtdf.de
→ Fotofestival Horizonte Zingst – www.horizonte-zingst.de
→ Fotofestival Mannheim Ludwigshafen Heidelberg – www.fotofestival.info
→ Fotosommer Stuttgart – www.fotosommer-stuttgart.de
→ Kunst Zürich – www.kunstzuerich.ch
→ Kunstmesse Salzburg – www.kunstmesse-salzburg.at
→ PARIS PHOTO – www.parisphoto.fr
→ photokina – www.photokina.de
→ Rencontres d'Arles – www.rencontres-arles.com
→ Sony World Photography Awards – www.worldphotographyawards.org
→ VIENNAFAIR – www.viennafair.at

(II.3.4) —— ASSOCIATIONS

→ BFF Bund Freischaffender Foto-Designer e.V. – www.bff.de
→ Bundesverband der Pressebild-Agenturen und Bildarchive e.V. (BVPA) – www.bvpa.org
→ CV CentralVerband Deutscher Berufsfotografen – www.cvfoto.de
→ Mittelstandsgemeinschaft Foto-Marketing (MFM) – www.mittelstandsgemeinschaft-foto-marketing.de
→ Verwertungsgesellschaft BILD-KUNST r.V. – www.bildkunst.de

(II.3.5) —— EDUCATION AND TRAINING

Training establishments
→ Berlin: Best-Sabel Berufsfachschule – www.best-sabel.de
→ Berlin: FOCON Innung der Fotografen –

- www.focon-international.eu
- → Berlin: Lette-Verein Fotodesign – www.lette-verein.de
- → Berlin: Photoacademy Urbschat – www.photoacademy.de
- → Berlin: Zentrum für Fotografische Ausbildung (ZFFA) – www.zffa.de
- → Bielefeld: Fachhochschule des Mittelstands – www.fhm-mittelstand.de
- → Bremen: Fachoberschule für Gestaltung – www.schule.bremen.de/schulen/huchting/fos/fos.html
- → Dresden: ESB mediencollege – www.mediencollege.de
- → Freiburg: Gertrud-Luckner-Gewerbeschule – www.glg-freiburg.de
- → Kiel: Photo + Medienforum Kiel – www.photomedienforum.de
- → Munich: BSZ Alois Senefelder – www.senefelder.musin.de
- → Oldenburg: Fotografen-Ausbildung bei CeWe Color – www.cewecolor.de
- → Pforzheim: Privatschule für Foto-Design – www.foto-design-schule.de
- → Stuttgart: Johannes-Gutenberg-Schule – www.jgs-stuttgart.de
- → Stuttgart: Lazi Akademie – www.lazi-akademie.de

Degree courses
- → Berlin – Berliner Technische Kunstschule – www.htk-berlin.de
- → Berlin: design akademie berlin – www.design-akademie-berlin.de
- → Berlin: Hochschule für Technik und Wirtschaft – www.htw-berlin.de
- → Bielefeld: Fachhochschule Bielefeld – www.fh-bielefeld.de
- → Bremen: Hochschule für Künste – www.hfk-bremen.de
- → Dortmund: Fachhochschule Dortmund – www.fh-dortmund.de
- → Duisburg-Essen: Universität Duisburg-Essen – www.folkwang-uni.de
- → Frankfurt: Städelschule – www.staedelschule.de
- → Furtwangen: Fakultät Digitale Medien – www.dm.hs-furtwangen.de
- → Hamburg: HFBK Hochschule für bildende Künste – www.hfbk-hamburg.de
- → Hannover: Fachhochschule Hannover – www.fotostudenten.de
- → Cologne: Fachhochschule – www.f07.fh-koeln.de
- → Cologne: Rheinische Fachhochschule – www.rfh-koeln.de
- → Krefeld: Hochschule Niederrhein – www.designkrefeld.de
- → Leipzig: Hochschule für Grafik und Buchkunst – www.hgb-leipzig.de
- → Munich: Macromedia Hochschule – www.macromedia-fachhochschule.de
- → Münster: Fachhochschule – www.fh-muenster.de
- → Nürnberg: Georg-Simon-Ohm-Hochschule – www.cgiatphotokina.de
- → Potsdam: Fachhochschule Potsdam – www.design.fh-potsdam.de
- → Stuttgart: Hochschule der Medien – www.hdm-stuttgart.de

(II.4) — INDEX

A
Accessories 30, 92, 160, 196, 248, 280
Adams, Ansel 37
Administration costs 258
Aliasing 105, 272
Analogue architectural photography 103, 209, 244
Analogue-to-digital convertor 272
Angle mirror 272
Angle of view 54, 98, 109, 173, 272
Animal photography 98
Anti-Scheimpflug 80, 272
Aperture 10, 55, 64, 71, 80, 97, 136, 169, 173, 178, 275
Archiving 219, 281
Artificial light 92, 136, 139, 149, 160, 163, 199, 224, 248
Asymmetrical layout 179, 183
Atget, Eugène 30, 33, 46

B
Bauhaus 38, 41, 45
Bayard, Hippolyte 19
Becher, Bernd 46, 48
Becher, Hilla 46, 48
Bellotto, Bernardo 17
Black point 197, 272, 276
Black value 228, 272
Blended light 163, 272
Blossfeldt, Karl 38, 42
Bogayevsky, N. V. 21
Brightness 55, 99, 108, 136, 163, 166, 196, 224, 248

C
Calibration 224, 249, 272
Calotype 20
Camera obscura 16, 19
Camera viewpoint 173, 177
Car photography 92
Centre filter 272
Centrefold 105, 272
Chevojon, Albert 25
Chromatic aberration 55, 199, 208, 249, 272
Chromaticity diagram 272
Circular level 111, 244, 248, 272
Coburn, Alvin Langdon 33
Colorimeter 228, 272
Colour 45, 66, 105, 108, 136, 163, 169, 199, 224, 249
Colour cast 105, 199, 248, 272,
Colour fringe 105, 201, 208, 272
Colour interpolation 108, 273
Colour space 169, 224, 273
Colour temperature 137, 149, 160, 169, 224, 273, 280
Colour temperature meter 163, 273
Composing 118, 179, 234, 273
Computer-generated imaging 234, 273
Contrast 63, 66, 108, 137, 169, 196, 228, 248
Copyright 254, 263, 266, 273
Corrections 60, 71, 136, 163, 178, 196, 201, 224, 245
Cropping 42, 54, 208, 249

D
Daguerre, Louis Jacques Mandé 19, 29, 37
Daguerreotype 19, 23
Delamotte, Philip Henry 22, 25
Depth of field 37, 57, 68, 71, 80, 136, 178, 273
Developing 196, 225, 248
Diffuse exterior light 137, 155
Diffuse light 45, 137
Digital architectural photography 103, 209, 244
Digital backs 10, 55, 95, 97, 102, 105, 108, 160, 169, 196, 244, 280
Digital technical camera 196
Distance from the subject 54, 173, 268
Distortion 25, 41, 54, 57, 93, 103, 201, 208, 245, 273
dpi 169, 197, 273
Dramatic lighting 33, 149, 152
Drawing with light 136
Dual Scheimpflug 80, 273
Durandelle, Louis-Émile 25

E
Eastman, George 28
Edison, Thomas A. 28
Endoscopy camera 236
Equipment 20, 26, 90, 95, 98, 108, 117, 163, 196, 224, 236, 242, 254, 280
Evans, Frederick Henry 29
Evans, Walker 41
Exposure metering 166
Extreme panorama 187

F
Fashion photography 71, 92, 105
File format 169
File size 169
Filter 27, 105, 136, 152, 160, 196, 224, 245, 280
Finishing 196, 208, 281
Flash equipment 236, 245, 280
Flash generator 153, 245
Flash system 245, 280
Focal length 54, 60, 71, 95, 108, 173, 244, 272
Focus cloth 135
Food photography 92
Framing 57, 209, 281
Fresnel lens 135, 248, 273
Fresnel, Augustin Jean 135, 273
Frontal perspective 25, 54, 66, 93

G
Gamma value 228, 274
Golden Ratio 179, 191
Goupil-Fesquet, Frédéric 23
Grey scale chart 199, 201, 224
Gropius, Walter 38

284

H
Häusser, Robert 45
Heliography 19
High dynamic range imaging 64
High dynamic range technology 137, 280
High-key photography 199, 274
High-quality print 68, 197
Histogram 99, 166, 197, 199, 274
Horizontal lines 60, 119, 212

I
Image circle 55, 62, 80, 93, 97, 105, 274
Image editing 196, 199, 224
Image format 54, 95, 98, 108, 160, 178, 197
Image processing software 92, 108, 169, 249, 280
IT-8 228, 274

J
Japonisme 33
JPEG format 169, 199

K
Kandinsky, Wassily 41
Klee, Paul 41
Kodak camera 29, 95, 196, 248, 280

L
Laboratory 55, 63, 196, 199, 209, 224, 230, 248, 280
Landscape format 45, 55, 178, 182
Landscape photography 8, 92, 105, 136
Large-format camera 46, 54, 93, 108, 274, 276
Lens hood 108, 248, 274
Light direction 136, 149, 152, 160
Light measurement 274
Lighting 66, 92, 117, 136, 149, 160, 199, 219, 224, 280
Lissitzky, El 38
Low-key photography 274

M
Manual spotlights 236, 274
Marketing 256, 260, 281
Microlens array 105, 275
Microstock agency 11, 234, 256, 260, 275
Model photography 71, 234
Moholy-Nagy, László 38, 45
Moholy, Lucia 41
Moiré effect 105, 199, 208, 244, 249, 275
Monitor 66, 99, 102, 208, 225, 248
Motion blur 97, 275

N
Negative film 20, 63, 137, 197, 224, 228, 248, 275
Negative plates 20, 196
Neue Sachlichkeit 30, 37, 41
Nièpce, Joseph Nicéphore 14, 19
Normal focal length 54, 60, 173, 244, 275
Normal lens 54, 93, 103, 244, 280

O
Object measurement 275
Object plane 275
Operating costs 258
Optical axis 54, 71, 93, 272
Optical bench 97, 244, 275

P
Panorama camera 188, 209
Parallax errors 59, 275
People photography 64, 92, 105, 139
Personal right 266
Perspective 16, 54, 57, 60, 93, 234, 259
Perspective correction 57, 60, 95, 136, 201, 249, 276
Peterhans, Walter 41
Photogrammetry 234, 275
Photographic discipline 92, 149, 201, 243, 254
Photographic paper 19, 26, 29, 57, 68, 178, 196, 208, 219, 228, 249
Photographic right 266
Photojournalism 92
Pictorialism 26, 32
Picture agency 259, 275
Portrait photography 8, 30, 37, 41, 60, 65, 71, 92, 110, 178, 254, 257
PostScript format 197, 275
Preparatory costs 258
Press photography 92, 256
Printer 66, 169, 224, 228, 249
Product photography 71, 92, 149, 236, 254

R
Rapid slide changer 275
RAW converter 249
RAW format 9, 55, 66, 137, 160, 169, 199, 220
Real-time histogram 99
Refraction blurring 71, 80, 275
Renger-Patzsch, Albert 38, 42
Resolution 55, 68, 93, 105, 169, 244, 275
Retouching 26, 99, 196, 201, 234
Retrofocus lens 97, 105, 275
Rodtschenko, Alexander 38
Rotation 57, 111, 201, 249

S
Scan back 276
Scanner 103, 197, 228, 248, 274, 280
Scanning software 248, 280
Scheimpflug principle 10, 54, 57, 71, 80, 136, 178, 276
Scheimpflug, Theodor 71, 276
Schmölz, Karl-Hugo 45
Sensor size 98, 108
Sharpness 20, 34, 68, 80, 93, 97, 102, 178, 199, 245
Sheeler, Charles 37, 41
Shift lens 54, 57, 93, 244
Shifting 57, 62, 80, 85, 136, 208, 244, 276
Shoot plan 119

Shulman, Julius 41
Single-lens reflex camera (SLR camera) 119
Skidmore, Owings and Merrill (SOM) 38
Slide film 63, 108, 136, 196, 225
Small-format camera 54, 57, 92, 97, 102, 119, 244
Softbox 153
Sports photography 92
Steichen, Edward 33
Steinert, Otto 45
Stereoscope 20
Stieglitz, Alfred 26, 34, 37
Stitching 55, 276
Stoller, Ezra 41
Straight photography 34, 37, 41
Strand, Paul 34, 37
Swinging 57, 71

T

Talbot, William Henry Fox 19
Telephoto lens 54, 57, 60, 92, 97, 108, 173, 244, 276
Test chart 81
TIFF format 169, 197, 201, 220
Tilting 57, 71, 80, 244
Tonal range 197, 276
Tripod 55, 64, 93, 97, 109, 117, 149, 160, 163, 248, 280
Tripod head 110, 248, 281

U

Using lines 41, 60, 179

V

Vanishing point 41, 57, 60, 276
Vernet , Emile-Jean-Horace 23
Vertical lines 41, 57, 136, 182, 208
View camera 10, 57, 60, 71, 80, 95, 102, 109, 119, 135, 169, 196, 244, 248, 276, 280
View lens 245, 280

W

White balance 169, 224, 230, 276
White point 197, 276
Wide-angle bellows 101, 248
Wide-angle lens 54, 57, 92, 95, 105, 173, 244

X

XY camera 244, 276

Z

Zille, Heinrich 30
360-degree panorama 52, 57

The *Deutsche Bibliothek* lists this publication in the *Deutsche Nationalbibliografie*. Detailed bibliographic data are available in the Internet at *http://dnb.ddb.de*

ISBN 978-3-86922-194-6

Original edition (German):
© 2010 by *Verlagsgruppe Hüthig Jehle Rehm GmbH*, Heidelberg et al.

Advanced licensed edition (German and English):
© 2012 by *DOM publishers*, Berlin
www.dom-publishers.com

This work is subject to copyright. All rights are reserved, whether the whole or part of the material is concerned, specifically the rights of translation, reprinting, recitation, broadcasting, reproduction on microfilms or in other ways, and storage or processing in data bases. Sources and owners of rights are stated to the best of our knowledge; please signal any we have might omitted.

Proofreading
Mariangela Palazzi-Williams
MPW Publishing Services, Richmond, Surrey/UK

Design
Nicole Wolf, Berlin

Printing
Tiger Printing (Hongkong) Co. Ltd.

Picture Sources and Acknowledgements
For photographs, model pictures, advice, information and other support, the authors and publishers would like to thank Dr. Bruno Dix (lawyer), the Library of Congress and the following companies: Alpa, Acra-Swiss, Bogen Imaging, Citrus3D Architekturvisualisierungen, Eizo, Epson, FOBA AG, GOSSEN Foto- und Lichtmesstechnik GmbH, Hasselblad, HENSEL Studiotechnik GmbH & Co. KG, Ingenieurbüro Marie A. Höreth, JOBO AG, Jos. Schneider Optische Werke GmbH, kranz (big print factory gmbh Sinzig), LaserSoft Imaging AG, Linhof Präzisions-Systemtechnik GmbH Munich, Manfrotto, Phase One, QUATOGRAPHIC Technology GmbH, Rodenstock Fotooptik LINOS Photonics GmbH & Co. KG, Sander Digital Pictures GmbH Cologne, Sinar Photography AG, Zörk Film & Fototechnik. Other images – if not indicated otherwise – courtesy of Axel Hausberg *(www.axelphoto.de)*.

Photographs on pages 22, 24, 28, 31, 32, 35, 36, 39 and 44 have been made available by the Archiv für Kunst und Geschichte; photographs on pages 21 and 27 by the Library of Congress, photograph on page 43 by the Bauhaus-Archiv Berlin; photograph on page 48 by the Fotoarchiv Ruhr Museum. All other historical photographs are in the public domain according to German copyright law. They are available in the Internet at *commons.wikimedia.org/wiki*.

Photograph on the cover by Stefan Müller.